# Triple-Entry Bookkeeping
## and
## Income Momentum

# Triple-Entry Bookkeeping
# and
# Income Momentum

**Yuji Ijiri**
*Carnegie-Mellon University*

iv

**To Taminosuke Nishimura**

*On His Seventy-Seventh Birthday*

# AMERICAN ACCOUNTING ASSOCIATION

The By-Laws of the American Accounting Association state that the first purpose of the Association shall be "to initiate, encourage, and sponsor research in accounting and to publish or aid in the publication of the results of research." In harmony with this objective, the publication of the Studies in Accounting Research is aimed at encouraging and publishing research. This series is an outgrowth of the research program initiated by the Association in 1965. Under this program research projects and authors are selected by the Director of Research, who is assisted by a Research Advisory Committee.

When the project is commissioned, the author is allowed maximum freedom in conducting research. The author is solely responsible for the procedures followed and the research conclusions.

This project was commissioned by A. Rashad Abdel-khalik (University of Florida), Director of Research. The Research Advisory Committee at that time was composed of A. Rashad Abdel-khalik (University of Florida), Andrew D. Bailey, Jr. (University of Minnesota), William L. Ferrara (Pennsylvania State University), Robert Libby (University of Michigan), James C. McKeown (University of Illinois at Champaign-Urbana), James A. Ohlson (University of California - Berkeley), and Thomas H. Williams (University of Wisconsin - Madison.)

**Table of Contents**

## LIST OF TABLES

# PREFACE

Is double-entry bookkeeping "absolutely perfect" as it has been claimed? Would it not be possible to extend it logically to triple-entry bookkeeping? If so, what would be the dimension that is destined to become the third dimension in the triple-entry system?

These are the questions that fascinated the author for more than a quarter century. Discussions and partial answers to some related questions on this double-entry problem have been published in his articles and monographs (1966 [14], 1967 [15], 1975 [17], and 1981 [19].) This monograph presents a solution to a "half" of the double-entry problem.

It is trivial to add an arbitrary third dimension and call it triple-entry bookkeeping, since if anything can appear as the third dimension, there is no room for theory, even if the resulting system is useful from a practical standpoint. The essential requirement for a solution to the double-entry problem is, therefore, that the third dimension must be logically deducible from the existing two dimensions (the debit and the credit) of double-entry bookkeeping.

In this monograph, the dichotomy of the double-entry bookkeeping system is critically examined to find the logic that binds the existing two dimensions. It is then shown that this dichotomy in the existing system is in fact an imperfect subset of a natural trichotomy upon which a system of triple-entry bookkeeping can be constructed. An examination of this new system, however, reveals that it is deficient in one major aspect. This in turn leads to still a newer type of triple-entry bookkeeping which indeed extends bookkeeping from a two-dimensional space to a three-dimensional space. Some new accounts and new forms of statements are examined along with their implications to financial reporting and accountability. At the end of the monograph, it is pointed out that the monograph solves only a half of the double-entry problem since there remains another half of double-entry bookkeeping that seems to defy any attempt to extend it logically to a triple-entry system.

The author is indebted to the 1981-82 Research Advisory Committee of the American Accounting Association, consisting of Professors A. Rashad Abdel-khalik (Chairman and the AAA Director of Research), Andrew D. Bailey, Jr., William L. Ferrara, Robert Libby, James C. McKeown, James A. Ohlson, and Thomas H. Williams, for their helpful comments and suggestions on an earlier draft of the monograph. In particular, detailed comments on various parts of the manuscript by Professor Abdel-khalik were most useful. The author is also indebted to Sara Toney for her careful editing of the monograph.

Needless to say, the author is solely responsible for any remaining errors and flaws in the monograph.

# 1. The Logic Behind Double-Entry Bookkeeping

## 1.1 Perfectness of Double-Entry Bookkeeping

Double-entry bookkeeping has been praised by many notable authors in history. In *Wilhelm Meister*, Goethe [12] states, "What advantage does he derive from the system of bookkeeping by double-entry! It is among the finest inventions of the human mind" (Book I, Volume I, Chapter X, p. 28). Arthur Cayley [5], a nineteenth century mathematician, calls the principle of bookkeeping by double-entry "like Euclid's theory of ratios an absolutely perfect one" (p. v). Similarly, a German economic historian, Werner Sombart [37] states, "... double-entry bookkeeping is borne of the same spirit as the system of Galileo and Newton" (Volume 2, Part 1, p. 119).

The landmark publication on double-entry bookkeeping is, needless to say, Luca Pacioli's [30] *Summa de Arithmetica, Geometria, Proportione et Proportionalita* (Everything Concerning Arithmetic, Geometry and Proportion), published in Venice in 1494. It seems to have been well established, however, that the practice of double-entry bookkeeping had existed more than a century before Pacioli. Peragallo [33] states, "The first to write on double-entry was probably Benedetto Cotrugli, [who] finished his book on the 25th of August, 1458..." (p. 54). But the practice of double-entry bookkeeping appears to have existed as early as 1340 in Genoa (Peragallo [33], Abs [1].) In any event, ever since it was developed, the basic framework of double-entry bookkeeping has remained unchanged for more than five centuries. Littleton [26] remarks that

> From the very beginning - say before the middle of the fifteenth century - certain basic peculiarities have been associated with double entry. These fundamental characteristics still persist and form the principal means of setting bookkeeping apart from other fact-manipulating systems. A characteristic technical manner of operating is one of the peculiarities which has undergone no basic change with the passing centuries.

Why is this so? Is this because double-entry bookkeeping is "absolutely perfect" in its internal logic, leaving no room for improvement or expansion ever since it was originally generated?

If double-entry bookkeeping is absolutely perfect, it can be understood why there has been no extension of it into *triple-entry bookkeeping*. A hypothesis which may be called the *perfectness hypothesis* of double-entry bookkeeping (that double-entry bookkeeping is perfect and cannot be extended to triple-entry bookkeeping without destroying its internal logic), seems to have been accepted explicitly or implicitly over a long period of time.

In other fields of science, the longer a hypothesis is accepted, the more challenging it is to disprove it. The same is certainly true with this perfectness hypothesis in accounting. What does it take if one is to show that double-entry bookkeeping is imperfect and indeed extensible into triple-entry bookkeeping?

Two conditions must be satisfied, *preservation of the old system* and *integrity of the new system.* First, to call a system an "extension" of an original system, the extended system must preserve everything that existed in the original system. For example, when the field of natural numbers was extended to the field of rational numbers, to the field of real numbers, and to the field of complex numbers, every extended field preserved elements and operations defined in the original field. Otherwise, the new system is not an extension of the old system.

The integrity of an extended system requires that the new dimension added to the old system must be logically and uniquely derived from the old dimensions and thus form an integral part of the dimensions of the new system.

While the preservation condition is relatively easy to verify by comparing the new and old systems, the integrity condition cannot be judged unless the basis for old dimensions is first identified. For example, after the sequence of integers 1 and 2, whether 3 should follow or 4 should follow would depend upon how the relation between the first two numbers is interpreted. If 2 were derived by adding 1 to the first number, then 3 should be the third number, while if 2 were derived by doubling the first number, then 4 should be the third number. Thus, depending upon how old dimensions are interpreted, the integrity condition may be fulfilled under one interpretation but not under another; however, the integrity condition requires that for any given interpretation the new dimension must be uniquely derived from the old ones.

The task needed to disprove the perfectness hypothesis is, therefore, to find a suitable way of interpreting the existing two dimensions of double-entry bookkeeping. Under the interpretation, there should be a unique dimension that logically follows from the existing two dimensions.

Unfortunately, the two dimensions in double-entry bookkeeping, the debit and the credit, contain numerous phases, most of which have no logical ways of being extended to three. If these phases are properly aligned, however, the possibility of, or even the need for, a third dimension might become evident, just like a proper positioning of the sun, the moon, and the earth creates an unusual view of the sun's coronas under an eclipse.

## **1.2** Multiple-Entry Bookkeeping: A Case of Failure

The dichotomy of double-entry bookkeeping is normally expressed in a double-entry equation:

$$\textbf{Assets} = \textbf{Liabilities} + \textbf{Capital} \qquad (1)$$

or, defining equities as the sum of liabilities (creditors' equity) and capital (owners' equity):

$$\textbf{Assets} = \textbf{Equities} \qquad (2)$$

Here, the equality sign is used as a shorthand to mean that the sum of the amounts of all items on its left is equal to the sum of the amounts of all items on its right. It is also used to represent that in abstract the left-side concept is contrasted with the right-side concept.

The two dimensions in equation 2, assets and equities, are said to represent the physical-economic properties of resources of an enterprise on one hand (assets), and the claims on those resources on the other hand (equities). Since the two dimensions are merely different ways of classifying the same set of resources, the two sums are equal by definition.

This way of understanding double-entry bookkeeping has been most widely accepted in accounting. For example, in one of his earliest writings, Paton (1917) [31] contrasts property (another name used for assets) and equities:

> The double-entry system of keeping accounts is founded logically in the nature of the facts with which accounting deals. These data consist fundamentally of the two classes, property and equities (rights in property). These two classes are always numerically equal, for one class consists of the objective items of property, the other class represents the situs of the ownership of this property, and the same measuring unit is used in both cases. The essence of the double-entry system is the separation of the members of the equation - property equals equities - and the maintenance of this equation. Thus the double-entry method is more than the mere recording of facts. The first step in the interpretation of data is made in the forming of the two fundamental classes (p. 25).

Essentially this view of double-entry bookkeeping considers it as a means for generating *double classification*. Double classification has a natural tie with a matrix representation of accounts and journal entries, as has been explored in a number of articles starting with Kohler's (1952) [25] notion of spread sheet and Mattessich's (1957) [29] matrix accounting.

However, if the double-entry equation arises because of classifying a given set of items in two ways, there seems to be no reason why the dimensions should be limited to two. In fact, there have been a couple of proposals to extend double-entry bookkeeping by adding new dimensions. Writing for a tax journal, Johnson (1963) [21, 22] suggested to add a third column in journal entries which is dedicated to computing taxable income. More generally, it was elaborated in Ijiri (1966 [14], 1967 [15], and 1975 [17]) that multiple-entry bookkeeping systems can easily be developed by introducing, in addition to the property and the claim dimensions, such other dimensions as the locations of the resources, the age of the resources, the organizational units which control the resources, etc. Examples of journal entries as well as financial statements that may be prepared from such a system have been elaborated in these publications.

Suppose, for example, that an enterprise was established with $50 in cash. Suppose further that it borrowed $30 in cash, and purchased a three-year old plant for $60. The plant was located in Canada and was placed under the control of its production department. In addition, $10 cash was remitted to Canada as a part of the plant management fund. These transactions may be recorded in quintuple entry and the resulting balance sheet may be presented as in the table that follows.

**Table 1-1:** Balance Sheet under Quintuple Entries

| Property | | Claim | | Location | | Age | | Control | |
|---|---|---|---|---|---|---|---|---|---|
| Cash | | $20 | Loan | $30 | Canada | $70 | Current | $20 | Prod. | $70 |
| Plant | | 60 | Capital | 50 | U.S. | 10 | 3YrOld | 60 | H.Q. | 10 |
| | | $80 | | $80 | | $80 | | $80 | | $80 |

Such a system of multiple-entry bookkeeping would be fine, were it not for the requirement of integrity. Unfortunately, on the question of integrity, the dimensions selected here fall apart. Why should Location be the dimension that follows Property and Claim? Why should the taxable income be the third dimension and not something else?

This is what makes this type of multiple-entry bookkeeping not very attractive from the theoretical standpoint, although in practice it may in fact be useful to add columns for income tax determination, for segment reporting, for inflation accounting, or for human resources.


## 1.3 Logic to Reduce Alternatives

Why is the integrity of the system so important? Would it not be important for accountants to have the flexibility of being able to choose whatever dimensions useful for given information needs?

Flexibility may be desirable from the standpoint of individual enterprises, but standardization is essential from the standpoint of the accounting system in an economy. Without standards an accounting system fails to function, just as a language system falls apart when each individual in a community speaks in his or her own flexible manner without standards.

In fact, the history of accounting seems to be the history of an endeavor to standardize accounting practice. A struggle to develop and maintain standards is evident not only in official pronouncements of rule-making bodies in accounting, but also in the early literature on accounting theory. For example, the efforts by the 1936 Executive Committee of the American Accounting Association, led by then President Eric Louis Kohler, resulted in a publication, "A Tentative set of Accounting Principles Affecting Corporate Reports," [2], which is perhaps the earliest such publication by an accounting organization to lay ground rules for accounting measurement and financial reporting. (Kohler's continual effort to standardize accounting resulted in the first publication of an accounting dictionary, his *Dictionary for Accountants*, published in 1952 [25].) Basic postulates discussed in Paton and Littleton's *An Introduction to Corporate Accounting Standards*, published by the American Accounting Association in 1940 [32], are also one of the earliest attempts to build accounting on a logical basis so that alternatives can be narrowed, as much as possible, by logic and not by the accountants' discretion. This is because an alternative selected by logical arguments has a better chance of being accepted widely than an alternative chosen by someone's arbitrary preference, as emphasized in a review of Paton-Littleton's monograph [18].

Therefore, the alternatives for the third dimension must be narrowed logically before an attempt is made to extend double-entry bookkeeping. This is important not only from the standpoint of practice for the reason stated above, but also from the standpoint of theory construction, since if anything and everything is allowed to happen, there will be no room for theory. There has to be a convincing, logical reason why a particular dimension is "destined" to become the third dimension of the triple-entry bookkeeping system.

Since the kinds of multiple-entry bookkeeping shown above are not desirable because of the lack of integrity in the extended system, it is necessary to reexamine the double-entry equation 2 once again.

While the logical reason for the dichotomy between assets and equities is not apparent, some components such as receivables and payables do have a definitive contrast, one being the logical opposite of the other. Then, a question arises: Why do those that are clearly negative assets appear on the same side of the equation as those, such as owners' equity, that have no such apparent contrast with assets?

The reason for this may be attributed to accountants' aversion to negative numbers that seems to have existed at the time of the publication of Pacioli's *Summa*. It may, therefore, be worthwhile to take a short excursion into the topic of negativity avoidance in accounting.

## 1.4 Negativity Avoidance

In reviewing the history of accounting, accountants' aversion to negative numbers is evident in numerous places. Negative numbers are avoided by setting up a different column or a separate account in which negative numbers are grouped and recorded as positive. They are eventually netted with the balance of the positive column or the positive account before preparation of a financial statement.

Three reasons for this negativity avoidance might be considered. One is for control purposes. It is more effective from the control standpoint to monitor not just net balance but gross amounts of positive and negative entries separately. Therefore, sales and sales returns are recorded separately, properties and accumulated depreciation are controlled by separate accounts, and netting of treasury stock and capital stock is prohibited.

A second reason that might be considered is that mixed operations of additions and subtractions took much more time than additions alone, especially for our ancestors without the convenience of calculators and computers. Even with a calculator, it is faster to add entries in the positive column and those in the negative column separately and to make one subtraction at the end, than to add and subtract entries with mixed signs. Saving time must have been significant for our ancestors with only abacuses available at best.

A third reason, which is the most important of the three, is that double-entry bookkeeping was built on a mathematical theory that did not recognize negative numbers. Peters and Emery (1980) [34] point this out in a discussion of the role of negative numbers in the development of double-entry bookkeeping.

According to Cajori's book on history of mathematics [4], cited by Peters and Emery, the earliest reference to negative numbers is created by the Chinese in the first century A.D. who used red rods for positive numbers and black rods for negative numbers. Red rods are used for recording what others owed to the person and black rods for what the person owed to others. Cajori also states that Brahmagupta in India in A.D. 628 made use of the negative numbers to record debt, but the practice died out because powerful Omar Khayyam (A.D. 1045-1123) rejected the existence of negative numbers.

Citing Kline [24], Peters and Emery conclude:

> Thus, it appears that the concept of negative numbers appeared first in accounting rather than mathematics. It is interesting to observe that even after mathematicians accepted the theoretical existence of negative numbers, they continued to reject the idea of their having any purpose. For example, Descartes (1596-1650) accepted negative numbers in part, calling them "false roots" ... However, other notable figures such as Pascal (1623-1662) regarded the subtraction of 4 from 0 as utter nonsense ... Thomas Harriot (1560-1621) was the earliest mathematician to accept negative numbers completely, almost a century after Pacioli's *Summa* was published ... Pacioli, like other mathematicians of his time, did his utmost to avoid even the use of a symbol for minus, let alone a negative number. Addition was denoted by $p$, and equations were written to cause all coefficients to be positive. Although an occasional subtraction of a term appears in the *Summa*, there is no question that Pacioli rejected negative numbers (pp. 425-426).

## 1.5 Wealth and Capital

Attempts to avoid negative numbers may have clouded the dichotomy underlying double-entry bookkeeping. Therefore, let us examine the double-entry equation in its alternate form, that is

$$\textbf{Assets - Liabilities} = \textbf{Capital} \tag{3}$$

This may be expressed simply as

$$\textbf{Wealth} = \textbf{Capital} \tag{4}$$

where wealth is defined to be assets less liabilities.

This dichotomy may in fact be preferable to the dichotomy of assets and equities because liabilities are more closely related to assets, if the signs are set aside, than to capital. Paton [31], in the same article quoted above expressed his concern over putting liabilities and capital together, even though he supported the dichotomy of assets and equities:

> It might be urged that we are here setting up an equality that is not grounded in any logical classification of facts, but is rather artificially maintained

by including among the so-called equity items highly dissimilar things. It might be insisted that proprietorship and outside equities show no relationship; that proprietorship is what the company is worth, and other liabilities are what it owes; that proprietorship is elastic and outside claims are rigid (p. 11).

. Thus, the above equation relating wealth and capital may offer a better basis for understanding the dichotomy of double-entry bookkeeping in the pure form. In fact, Littleton [27] considers capital, or in his term "proprietorship," as the essential basis for double-entry. He states that "...the essential criterion of double-entry bookkeeping, as the term is now understood, is commercial proprietorship, and especially those elements which are called 'nominal accounts' or 'economic accounts'" (p. 27). He also emphasizes [28] that

> Without nominal accounts a coherent scheme of interrelated accounts converging into capital accounts would not be possible. Without this scheme, the operations that we now call double-entry bookkeeping could not be carried on, and statements designed to analyze the economic activities that constitute the reason for the existence of an enterprise could not be constructed (p. 352).

Based on the equality of wealth and capital, it is then possible to consider a bookkeeping system in which all changes in wealth are always recorded on one side (debit) and all changes in capital are always recorded on the other side (credit) of a journal entry. Nothing is lost by such a new system since the sign of a number, rather than its position in a journal entry, represents unambiguously what happened to the corresponding wealth or capital accounts. Furthermore, such a system may add clarity to the meaning of the journal entry, since one side of the entry handles only wealth and its changes while the other side handles only capital and its changes.

In any event, the wealth-capital dichotomy seems to offer a new perspective on the reason for putting two dimensions together. What would be the reason for contrasting wealth and capital? One answer might be that the wealth side is "real" while the capital side is "nominal" (or "abstract"). While such a characterization of accounts has been used in the past and is certainly a useful viewpoint, a difficulty arises when one tries to extend it to a trichotomy. Real, nominal, and what? Supernominal? (One might be able to come up with a new dimension that may correspond to the Holy Spirit in the Trinity, but this may require a religious insight into the fundamental nature of accounting!)

Perhaps the nature of wealth and capital may have to be examined in more depth in order to logically extend the dichotomy. Wealth is, as stated before, assets less liabilities; or more precisely, it consists of assets and liabilities whose measurements carry opposite signs. Capital is owners' equity and as such it includes retained earnings to which all income accounts in the past are closed. Capital also contains capital stock and additional paid-in capital which summarize all past contributions by the owners.

Both wealth and capital describe the financial status of a given enterprise at a given point in time. As of the date of the balance sheet, wealth describes the *present* state of the set of all resources, positive or negative, that belong to the enterprise, the term "present" being used here in reference to the date of the statement.

There may be a dispute over the statement that wealth represents the "present" financial status since some of the items such as receivables and payables await deliveries in the future, while some others are expressed in prices in the past. However, while a delivery may yet to be made in the future, a right to receive the delivery or an obligation to make the delivery exists presently on the statement date. A mixture of past and present prices may be used in the financial statements to describe resources, but the resources described are always something that belong to the enterprise presently on the statement date.

Therefore, it would be correct to regard the wealth side of the double-entry equation as a description of the present financial status of an enterprise. But then, would it not be the same on the capital side? Isn't owners' equity also a description of the present financial status of the enterprise, perhaps at a somewhat more abstract level than that used in the wealth side?

On the surface it may appear that the two sides of the double-entry equation must have the same time reference, since otherwise the two sides cannot be equal all the time. Yet there seems to be some difficulty in stating that capital accounts describe the present financial status of the enterprise.

This is because capital accounts are all intangibles which lack specific identification. The present status of such intangibles can be identified and described only by means of their past history. In fact, it may not be unreasonable to consider the purpose of capital accounts to lie in summarizing past events rather than describing the present status. If the past is properly accounted for, then cumulative past should equal present under a given measurement framework.

If necessary, wealth accounts could be prepared by taking inventories of all assets and liabilities of an enterprise at a given point in time, and by applying whatever prices may be available and appropriate at that time, without knowing the past records of the enterprise. There is no way that such an approach can be taken in the case of capital accounts.

If this point of view on the role of capital accounts is acceptable, then a rather clear dichotomy between wealth and capital emerges. Wealth accounts keep track of assets and liabilities of an enterprise at "present," while capital accounts keep track of their changes in the "past." These are not changes in individual asset and liability accounts since they are too numerous, but changes in the amount of aggregate wealth (or net worth as it has been often referred to), classifying them based on why and when such an increase or a decrease has occurred.

## **1.6** Present Being Accounted for by the Past

Capital accounts, including all income accounts in the past which are in essence subaccounts of retained earnings, are thus oriented toward describing the past while wealth accounts are oriented toward describing the present of the enterprise. When the two are equal in the aggregate amount, then it becomes possible to say that *the present is fully accounted for by the past*, or expressing this point concisely,

$$\textbf{Present} = \textbf{Past} \qquad (5)$$

This interpretation of double-entry bookkeeping gives a good insight into the significant contribution made by double-entry bookkeeping over single-entry bookkeeping. The contribution brought by double-entry bookkeeping is often trivialized as a computational check for reducing errors by entering the same number twice. Far from it. While in single-entry bookkeeping the present status of an enterprise is presented merely as such by a set of wealth accounts only, double-entry bookkeeping forces people to "account for" the present status by a suitable set of capital accounts that captures the past events that led to the present status. *Accountability* is thus at the heart of the double-entry bookkeeping system.

Think of what happens to accountability when the linkage between the present and the past is broken. An enterprise collects $10 million of shareholders' money and engages in a project. At the end of the project, the management returns $3 million to the shareholders indicating that this is all the management could recoup from the project. The shareholders would most likely demand an explanation. By that they mean an accounting for the past events that led to the shrinkage of the original $10 million to $3 million. No matter how honest the management may be, they have not accounted for the loss if all they can say is that the original investment of $10 million has somehow shrunk mysteriously to $3 million. This lack of accountability which can easily occur in the single-entry system cannot occur in the double-entry system without deliberately falsifying the entries.

Even more importantly, under the double-entry system this accounting for the present by the past is done, not casually and haphazardly, but *systematically and completely*, since otherwise the two sides do not balance. It is this pressure placed upon managers and accountants to be accountable for wealth changes that is the most fundamental contribution of the double-entry bookkeeping system.

It is perhaps unfair to give an impression that accountability was completely lacking in the single-entry bookkeeping era. In fact, it appears that there was a fairly sophisticated system of "tablets" on possessions, purchases, expenditures, and so on, even in the Mesopotamian era which must have contributed greatly to enforcing some degree of accountability (Keister [23]). Similarly, an elaborate accounting control system appears to have existed in Greece since the fifth century B.C. (Hain [13]). Furthermore, the system of bookkeeping in the Middle Ages had reached a fairly advanced level shortly before the introduction of double-entry bookkeeping as discussed in the history of accounting before Pacioli (deRoover [8, 9], Yamey [38]).

It is certainly true that a high level of an accountability system can be developed and maintained under single-entry bookkeeping if the system is carefully managed by a competent manager. Yet there is an enormous difference between an elementary system that could perform an advanced task if handled by competent persons and an advanced system that does such a task automatically. The double-entry bookkeeping system has the latter property which is the key feature that distinguishes it from the single-entry bookkeeping system.

# 2. Temporal Triple-Entry Bookkeeping

## 2.1 Past, Present, and Future

Once the dichotomy between wealth and capital is converted into a slightly more abstract one contrasting past and present, it is quite natural to extend the pair of concepts to a trichotomy of past, present, and *future*. Thus, a part of the task on hand has been accomplished, since the dichotomy in the conventional double-entry system has been captured in the form in which an extension to a trichotomy is obvious. The remaining task is to find out what such a system of triple-entry bookkeeping might look like, what kind of use such a system might have, and what form of financial statements such a system might imply.

A triple-entry equation which may be written as

$$\textbf{Future} = \textbf{Present} = \textbf{Past} \tag{6}$$

forms a basis for constructing a triple-entry system. For an obvious reason, such triple-entry bookkeeping will be referred to as *temporal* triple-entry bookkeeping to distinguish it from possible other triple-entry systems that may be generalized from different interpretations of the existing double-entry system. The new dimension to be added to the existing dimensions of wealth and capital will deal with budgeted, planned, or projected events of the enterprise and will be designated simply as "budget" so that the triple-entry equation may be given more descriptive appearance as in

$$\textbf{Budget} = \textbf{Wealth} = \textbf{Capital} \tag{7}$$

What is the meaning of the equality in equation 6 where Future is equated with Present? The equality between Past and Present in the double-entry system was interpreted as the present being fully accounted for by the past. An analogy suggests, then, that Future = Present might be interpreted as the future being fully accounted for by the present, but this would not work. This is because Present, being only a single point in time, does not have the capability of accounting for or explaining something. It can only be an object of explanation and not the source of explanation which ordinarily requires tracing of changes over time.

Thus, a proper way of taking the analogy might be the reverse, that is, Future = Present means the present being fully accounted for by the future. This does sound odd, since unless time flows in reverse, the future is not capable of accounting for the present, just as children cannot give birth to the parents. But let us persist on this line for a moment.

In the double-entry system the present status of an enterprise is accounted for by its past, but how far back in the past? Back to the inception of the enterprise since by linking all financial statements in the past, complete accounting since the inception of the enterprise is certainly possible. Would this mean that tracing "back" to the future, when time flows in reverse, must extend to the liquidation of the enterprise?  This would be very, very difficult.

It might be necessary, therefore, to limit the horizon, both toward the past and toward the future by an arbitrary means, such as an accounting period which is normally taken to be one year.  Then, as far as any given financial statements are concerned, Present = Past does not mean accounting for the present by the entire past history of the enterprise but only by the events that occurred during the most recent year in the past.  The history beyond that period is all summarized in the amount of "Beginning Capital" which provides a linkage between a given statement and its predecessors.

Applying this observation to the future dimension, entries in this dimension in any given statement will be limited to events that are expected to occur in the coming year only.  An amount analogous to the last year's beginning capital would then serve as a linkage between this statement and its successors.  What would such an amount represent?  That has to be what may be called "Target Capital"; what the enterprise expects to reach at the end of the coming year if its budgets are realized exactly.

This gives rise to an interesting observation.  Suppose that the enterprise's capital was $100 million a year ago, is $150 million now, and is budgeted to reach $200 million a year from now.  Then, Present = Past is shown on a statement as $150 = $100 + $50 (in millions), where $50 million is broken into various reasons for the capital to have reached $150 million from the beginning capital of $100 million.  The equality of the two dimensions is maintained in this way.  This means that in Future = Present the arithmetic should be $200 - $50 = $150 (in millions), so that the entire statement in triple entry would show $150 million in total in each of the three columns.  That is, budgeted income of $50 million must be *subtracted* from the target capital of $200 million in the newly added dimension.  Revenues are decreases and expenses are increases in capital in this dimension.

Then, it might make some sense to say that the present is accounted for by the future.  Using the target capital as an anchor, the budgeted activities for the coming year are "reconciled back" to the present status of the enterprise, while actual activities in the last year are "reconciled forward" to the present status, starting with the last year's beginning capital.

## **2.2** Types of Journal Entires

Now a picture of a new statement emerges gradually.  But what about day-to-day journal entries?  What would they look like in triple-entry bookkeeping?

Again, a careful examination of journal entries under the double-entry system is necessary before it is extended to the triple-entry system.  Earlier it was pointed out that the practice of transposing negative entries disturbed the purity of entries by mixing wealth and capital accounts in the same column merely to avoid negative numbers, and that nothing is lost by entering all entries to wealth accounts in one column and all entries to capital accounts in another column.  Thus, for example, a purchase of an inventory for $10 in cash can be recorded as "Cash -$10" and "Inventories $10," both appearing on debit with no credit entries. The sum of all debit entries (zero in this case) is still equal to the sum of all credit entries (also zero in this case) in every transaction.

Viewed in this manner, every transaction in the double-entry system may be classified into three categories: intra-wealth transactions, intra-capital transactions, and wealth-capital transactions.

Intra-wealth transactions are those that do not change total wealth but merely transfer an amount from one wealth account to another. Purchases in cash or on account, consumption of raw materials in production, lending and borrowing, collection of receivables or payment of payables -- all are intra-wealth transactions. Entries for such a transaction are all in the wealth column only, and the amounts of such entries always sum to zero.

Intra-capital transactions are those that do not change total capital but merely transfer an amount from one capital account to another. Stock dividends, conversions of convertible preferred stock, appropriation of retained earnings for reserves in the capital account, are all examples of intra-capital transactions. Entries for such a transaction are all in the capital column only, and the amounts of such entries always sum to zero.

Wealth-capital transactions are those that affect total wealth and total capital simultaneously. In addition to all transactions involving revenues, expenses, gains and losses, these transactions include new stock issues, stock retirements, treasury stock purchases or sales, and cash dividend declarations. Entries for such a transaction appear on both the wealth and capital columns, and the sum of the amounts of entries in each column must be equal.

An analogy then suggests that when the double-entry system is extended to the triple-entry system there should be a new category of transactions called "intra-budget transactions" which handles changes in the budgets. Entries for such a transaction are all in the budget column only, and the amounts of such entries always sum to zero. In addition, what was called "wealth-capital" transactions must now be called "budget-wealth-capital" transactions. This is because once a transaction increases or decreases total wealth it must simultaneously change the amount of total budget and total capital by the same amount in order to maintain the triple-entry equation, Budget = Wealth = Capital.

This point gives a clue on the meaning of an entry in the budget column. Suppose in the earlier example, where capital is at present $150 million but is expected to increase to $200 million by the end of the year, the enterprise earned $20 million and its capital at a mid-year point has increased to $170 million. The wealth column describes various assets and liabilities whose amounts sum to $170 million. The capital column starts with the beginning capital of $150 million but recognizes $20 million earned so far in income accounts, for the total of $170 million. This then means that the budget column which started out with a target capital of $200 million less $50 million budgeted income must now show $170 million in total. But how? Naturally, by reducing budgeted income from $50 million to $30 million. What does $30 million mean? Clearly it represents the amount of income yet to be earned.

Stated in accountability terms, the management accountability for the budgeted income of $50 million has been reduced to $30 million as a result of having earned $20 million up to now. At the end of the year, the balance (positive or negative) represents the variance between budget and actual on every budget account, reconciling the target capital established a year earlier to the capital actually achieved at the end of the year.

Having obtained some basic ideas on what journal entries and financial statements might look like under the triple-entry system, it will be useful to consider some examples of transactions and financial statements; this will be discussed in the next section.

## **2.3** An Example of Accounts and Journal Entries

To show how this triple-entry bookkeeping may be carried out by means of a simple example, consider a company which started on 1/1/x0 with $50 in cash. During the coming year, the company expects to borrow $40, to spend $80 to acquire a plot of land, to earn $30 in cash in rental income, and to spend $10 in cash for various expenses. Thus, the company's wealth at the end of the year is expected to be $70, consisting of cash $30, land $80, and loan -$40.

The company's wealth and capital accounts are both $50 as of 1/1/x0. Based on the plan, $70 is entered as Target Capital, from which $30 estimated rental income is deducted and $10 estimated expenses are added to arrive at the starting balance of $50, which equals total wealth and total capital at the beginning.

Thus, the beginning trial balance looks as shown in Table 2-1.

**Table 2-1:** Beginning Trial Balance

| Budget | | Wealth | | Capital | |
|---|---|---|---|---|---|
| Target Capital | $70 | Cash | $50 | Capital Stock | $50 |
| Est. Revenues | -30 | | | | |
| Est. Expenses | 10 | | | | |
| | | | | | |
| Total Budget | $50 | Total Wealth | $50 | Total Capital | $50 |

Suppose during the year, the company did exactly as planned, except that it earned $10 more in rent and spent $5 more for expenses than it originally planned. Journal entries for each of the transactions during the year may then be shown as in Table 2-2.

At the end of the year, then, the trial balance looks as shown in Table 2-3.

Note that the balances of accounts in the budget column all show the variances between budget and actual (positive being favorable, negative unfavorable), with the exception of Target Capital which stays at the estimated amount. At the beginning of next year, they are all substituted by a new set of

**Table 2-2:** Journal Entries

| | *Budget* | | *Wealth* | | *Capital* | |
|---|---|---|---|---|---|---|
| 1. Borrowing | | -: | Cash | $40: | | - |
| | | -: | Loan | -40: | | - |
| 2. Land Purchase | | -: | Land | 80: | | - |
| | | -: | Cash | -80: | | - |
| 3. Rental Income | Est. Rev. | $40: | Cash | 40: | Revenues | $40 |
| 4. Expenses | Est. Exp. | -15: | Cash | -15: | Expenses | -15 |

**Table 2-3:** Ending Trial Balance

| *Budget* | | *Wealth* | | *Capital* | |
|---|---|---|---|---|---|
| Target Capital | $70 | Cash | $35 | Capital Stock | $50 |
| Est. Revenues | 10 | Land | 80 | Revenues | 40 |
| Est. Expenses | -5 | Loan | -40 | Expenses | -15 |
| Total Budget | $75 | Total Wealth | $75 | Total Capital | $75 |

budgets and targets, while the balances of capital accounts are closed to retained earnings, with the exception of capital stock which remains unchanged.

Note that the entries in the budget and the capital columns in the journal entries are all mirror images of each other, although this may not be the case if, for example, the budget column is classified by projects' or departmental contributions to Target Capital. Then, the budget dimension accounts for projects' or departmental profit budgets and actual progress toward them.

## 2.4 Statement of Budget

Of course, in preparing a statement from budget accounts, a more informative set of descriptions may be used than those in account names in the trial balance; just as balance sheet, prepared from wealth accounts, and income statement and statement of owners' equity, prepared from capital accounts, are not just a listing of accounts. The signs in budget accounts may be properly adjusted so that the statement can be easily understood.

An example of statement of budget (or budget statement) is shown below. When such a statement can be incorporated as a part of regular financial statements, it would perhaps be more useful if a new set of budgets for the coming year is also reported alongside. Therefore, an example of this is also included in the last column.

It is particularly nice to realize that double-entry bookkeeping has the potential of being naturally and logically extended to include budgets, in view of

**Table 2-4:** Statement of Budget

|                          | Actual | Budget | Better -Worse | New Budget |
|--------------------------|--------|--------|---------------|------------|
| Beginning Owners' Equity | $ 50   | $ 50   | $ -           | $ 75       |
| Revenues                 | 40     | 30     | 10            | 60         |
| Cost of Sales            | -8     | -4     | -4            | -20        |
| Other Expenses           | -7     | -6     | -1            | -5         |
| Net Income               | 25     | 20     | 5             | 35         |
| Ending Owners' Equity    | $ 75   | $ 70   | $ 5           | $110       |

the fact that a number of authors have advocated the need for integrating budgets in financial statements.

For example, Cooper, Dopuch and Keller (1968) [6] state, *"Budgetary disclosure* as we employ the term refers both to (1) the published projection of next-period balance sheet, income and funds flow statements *and* (2) its critical comparison with actual results in a stockholders' report at the end of each period."  The above budget statement satisfies the two requirements if suitable explanations on the discrepancies are added in the footnotes to the statement. A similar form has also been examined in Ijiri (1968) [16] along with discussions on standards that may be needed if budgets are to be audited. Davidson (1972) [7] also proposes to use income and funds statements with three columns -- last year, this year and next year -- although he suggests to postpone balance sheet projections "until we have a better handle on the operating statements."

It is also interesting to note that in 1973 the Securities and Exchange Commission of the United States altered its position on filing of corporate projections completely, and decided not only to accept corporate projections of sales and earnings, but also to take steps to encourage their filings.

A temporal triple-entry system can certainly offer a basis upon which such proposals may be implemented systematically.

## **2.5** A Disappointment

All seems nice and neat with temporal triple-entry bookkeeping.  Theoretically, its trichotomy among past, present, and future seems perfect.  No other dimensions can be added to the group nor can be used to replace its member without destroying the logic that binds the triad.  From the practical standpoint, the usefulness in incorporating budgets seems to be evident both in internal and external accounting as has been elaborated in numerous articles on budgets.

However, there seems to be something missing in this triple-entry bookkeeping system.  When the double-entry system was introduced to accounting, it generated a whole new set of accounts that had not been developed under the single-entry system. It must have been as revolutionary as a "needleman," if we may refer to a creature in a single-dimensional world as such, suddenly exposed to a "flatland." If so, a move to a triple-entry system should be as revolutionary as a "flatman" suddenly exposed to a three-dimensional world. The new system ought to inject a whole new dimension into accounting. Yet, the set of budget accounts generated under the new system seems to be merely a mirror image of capital accounts already in existence.

In fact, it appears that the above triple-entry system is really not a triple-entry system but the double-entry system applied twice. It is an extension of the double-entry system to the other half space (the future as against the past) of the two-dimensional space, so to speak. The new system is still two-dimensional in spite of the fact that it has an appearance of being three dimensional. How disappointing!

Before going back to the original drawing board, however, it might be useful to review what went wrong in the above approach. The trouble lies in the fact that the new dimension in the temporal triple-entry system was not "created" but merely "copied" from the existing dimension by just changing its sign. This is certainly not a right approach. To create a third dimension, in the true sense of the word, the relationship between the first and the second dimensions must be extracted and applied to the relationship between the second and the third dimensions. Then, the third relates to the second in the same way as the second relates to the first. In the above triple-entry system, the third relates to the *first* in the same way as the second relates to the first. This is why no progress was made in developing an entirely new dimension.

This does not mean that temporal triple-entry bookkeeping should not be explored further. On the contrary, as will be emphasized later in the chapter on accountability, a temporal triple-entry system offers an important basis for relating budgets with existing financial statements and contains many aspects that are theoretically interesting and practically useful. Its only disappointing feature is that it does not extend the existing double-entry system toward a new dimension but merely toward the other half space in the existing dimension.

Let us, therefore, go back to the dichotomy of present and past and reexamine what the dichotomy really means.

# 3. Differential Triple-Entry Bookkeeping

## 3.1 Stock and Flow

It was pointed out, in passing, that present is a single point in time while past is a duration of time. The difference between the two might offer a basis for looking at the dichotomy in a new light. Wealth accounts represent the present financial status of an enterprise and, as such, they are all *stock* accounts. Capital accounts, on the other hand, represent the changes in wealth in the past, hence they are all *flow* accounts.

Thus, instead of contrasting present and past, it may be worthwhile to concentrate on the dichotomy between stock and flow. The double-entry equation,

$$\textbf{Stock} = \textbf{Flow} \tag{8}$$

may then be interpreted as the stock of wealth being fully accounted for by the flow of capital.

The trouble is that this dichotomy, like that of "real" and "nominal" mentioned earlier, seems to be very difficult to extend to a trichotomy, since the duality of stock and flow seems to be so natural and so frequently used as a pair of concepts.

But let us not give up so easily. What is the relationship between the stock and the flow? Clearly the flow means a change in the value of stock. The flow is determined as a result of recognizing a change in the value of stock at two points in time, say before and after an event or the beginning and the end of a period. If the stock changes its value continuously, then the flow may be considered as the "derivative" of the stock; namely, the rate of change in the stock variable.

If capital is a derivative of wealth (though this is a loose statement as will be discussed later), then would it not be possible to consider a derivative of capital? In calculus, a derivative of a derivative is not only possible but plays an important role in constructing higher dimensions. What would a derivative of capital really mean in accounting terms? It must have something to do with changes in an income and other capital account when its value in one period is compared with corresponding ones in one period earlier. Is there not a concept like that already in accounting? Yes, there is. The concept of "variance" deals with changes in income accounts.

For example, changes in revenues or expenses between this year and last year have been evaluated in variance analysis, classifying the discrepancy in various forms of variances, such as price variance, quantity variance, volume variance, etc. This is fortunate since, if the third dimension to be created is entirely foreign to accounting, the task would be enormously difficult.

However, even with the aid of existing concepts in variance analysis, the task of developing the third dimension is not easy. This is because variance analysis in the existing accounting system is carried outside the bookkeeping system and only on selected items or time periods. It is not an integral part of the bookkeeping system, at least not yet.

The situation is perhaps analogous to the situation before the introduction of the double-entry system. Concepts of revenues and expenses seem to have existed before the introduction of double-entry bookkeeping, but they had been isolated and had not been an integral part of the bookkeeping system. A contribution of the double-entry system is in pulling such isolated income concepts together and making them a systematic part of bookkeeping. Analogy then suggests that the triple-entry system must pull together various forms of variances, generalize them, and make them a systematic part of bookkeeping.

Over the centuries since the inception of the double-entry system, account-ants have developed an ingenious way of categorizing the reasons for changes in wealth. All income accounts are the result of numerous accountants' efforts to characterize the reasons for change in wealth, efforts perhaps comparable to the biologists' taxonomical efforts. Such efforts must now be directed toward characterizing reasons for increases or decreases in various income items, if this type of triple-entry bookkeeping is to succeed.

For convenience, let us designate this new type of bookkeeping *differential* triple-entry bookkeeping. The term "differential," as it is used here, reflects its mathematical meaning reasonably well. Capital, as stated above, may be viewed as a derivative of wealth in the sense that it reflects the change in wealth over time. However, from a measurement standpoint, capital is not exactly a derivative, since the derivative means rate of change. It is more like the rate of change multiplied by the length of time during which the change took place. In calculus, such a concept is called *differential*, the derivative multiplied by another variable (length of time, for example). It is also a useful feature that a differential of a function is in the same unit as the original one, since both wealth and capital must be measured in the same unit (and actually add to the same figure.)

## 3.2 Newtonian Mechanics

Although the concept of differential and other related concepts in calculus are useful in developing the differential triple-entry system, a field in which such concepts are used to describe empirical phenomena may offer a more concrete and useful basis by which the framework for the triple-entry system may be developed. Newtonian mechanics seems to offer a perfect basis for this endeavor.

As may be seen in any elementary physics book, the basic triple concepts that are used to describe the motion of an object are *position, velocity* and *acceleration*. Position $\mathbf{x}$ is measured with respect to a coordinate system which serves as a frame of reference. Velocity $\mathbf{v}$ is the rate of change in the position with respect to time $t$, namely, $\mathbf{v} = d\mathbf{x}/dt$. Acceleration $\mathbf{a}$ is the rate of change in the velocity with respect to time $t$, namely $\mathbf{a} = d\mathbf{v}/dt$.

Velocity and acceleration, together with the mass *m* of the object, determine *momentum* and *force*. Momentum **p** is mass times velocity, namely, $\mathbf{p} = m\mathbf{v}$. Force **F** is mass times acceleration, namely $\mathbf{F} = m\mathbf{a}$. From these various other concepts are defined such as impulse, work, kinetic and potential energy.

All these measurements, with the exception of mass, are functions of time and are of the same number of dimensions as that of the underlying coordinate system, hence the use of boldface which is a conventional way of representing vectors. The space is normally perceived to be three-dimensional, although there is a theory on a "curved" space which is considered to be four-dimensional.

One of the great contributions by Galileo and Newton is the concept and measurement of *force*. Force is a concept abstracted from the motion of objects and it plays the central role in Newtonian mechanics. "The essence of the Newtonian approach to mechanics is that the motion of a given object is analyzed in terms of the forces to which it is subjected by its environment," states French [11] in his book on Newtonian mechanics.

Relating this to the accounting framework, income and other components of the capital dimension, which describe changes in wealth, may be compared to momentum. Then, the concept that must be handled in the third dimension in the triple-entry system has to be the concept of *force*.

In order to develop the concept of force, it is necessary to understand the notion of income momentum. Under double-entry bookkeeping the concept of income has been well established but not the concept of income momentum, although the two are closely related. The income concept merely refers to the fact that the wealth of an enterprise was increased by the indicated amount as a result of its operations during a given period. Income momentum goes beyond the concept of income in the sense that it refers to the ability of the enterprise to keep generating income at the given rate. Then, force is perceived as a factor that influences this income momentum.

A business enterprise is subjected to various internal and external forces that collectively determine how income is changed from one period to next. While changes in income have been widely quoted in daily newspapers and business periodicals, such as a percentage increase in per-share income this year over last year, they have not been systematically identified with or attributed to the underlying forces that caused the change. This seems to be exactly what is needed in order to extend the double-entry system to the triple-entry system.

Admittedly, force is an unfamiliar term in accounting. However, the notion of *power* has been introduced in accounting many years ago, ever since the concept and measurement of "earning power" was introduced in some of the official pronouncements [3]. While earning power essentially refers to the income momentum of the enterprise, the concept of force goes one step further and explains the reason for the change, if any, in the income momentum. Therefore, let us use the term "force" as the basic concept upon which the third dimension in triple-entry bookkeeping is built.

Thus, we may now express the triple-entry equation as

$$\textbf{Wealth} = \textbf{Capital} = \textbf{Force} \qquad\qquad (9)$$

It is true that when wealth, capital, and force are contrasted, the middle term appears to be odd, since capital has too much static connotation. It would be nice to rename the second dimension as *income* and make the equation:

$$\textbf{Wealth} = \textbf{Income} = \textbf{Force} \qquad\qquad (10)$$

which relates the three concepts nicely, since force changes income which, in turn, changes wealth. Although income is not the only reason for the change in wealth, it is the principal reason for wealth change and is certainly appropriate to use as the name of the second dimension. However, since the concept of capital has already been widely accepted, its usage will be retained here as far as the name of the dimension is concerned, although, in terms of substance, the contrast will be made among wealth, income and force.

Note that while capital is a differential of wealth and while force is a differential of capital, an equality among them must hold, because of the above equation. This means that capital and force must be "integrated" back to arrive at the same wealth that is to be accounted for. As in calculus, this integration is done by using initial conditions; namely, conditions that existed at the beginning of the period in question.

## 3.3 A New Trial Balance

Let us again use the example of the company mentioned earlier. Since the details of the company's wealth (cash, land, loan) are not important in the argument, let us simplify by assuming that cash is the only wealth account and that the company has $120 in cash at the end of 19x2; it consists of $45 earned in 19x2 and $25 in 19x1, together with the $50 in cash with which the company started at the end of 19x0. Assuming no other transactions, cash balance at the end of 19x0, 19x1, and 19x2 are $50, $75, and $120, respectively.

Annual increases in cash balance are then accounted for by capital accounts. In this case $25 ($75 - $50) is attributed to activities in 19x1 and $45 ($120 - $75) to 19x2.

**Table 3-1:** Trial Balance with the Force Dimension

| Wealth | | Capital | | Force | |
|---|---|---|---|---|---|
| Cash | $120 | Capital Stock | $50 | Initial Balance | $50 |
| | | Income 19x1 | 25 | Force 19x1 | 50 |
| | | Income 19x2 | 45 | Force 19x2 | 20 |
| Total | $120 | Total | $120 | Total | $120 |

The force accounts reflect the fact that from the initial condition of $50, the company gained the momentum of earning at the rate of $25 a year. Over the two-year period, this momentum established in 19x1 earned the total of $50, which is attributed to Force 19x1. This is based on an assumption that income momentum lasts forever once it is established by a force. While this is unrealistic, this is done for the sake of simplicity in illustration. Later a notion of friction will be introduced.

During 19x2, the income momentum was increased from $25 a year to $45 a year, which means that the force applied in 19x2 resulted in $20 contributions to wealth by the end of 19x2. It may be seen then that the force accounts completely account for flow accounts and their changes during the years shown in Table 3-1.

## **3.4** Force Accounts

Once the basic nature of the force accounts is understood, it is easy to introduce variety of accounts in a manner analogous to various forms of variances. Each account will then show the impact of a particular factor such as a price change, a quantity change, or a volume change (effect of a change in the activity level on overhead allocation) upon revenue and expense flows.

For example, once there is a price increase in the product, an account for price force of the product may be established. Future earnings are then attributed to this force account as long as they are judged to originate from this price increase. Similarly, an account for quantity force or interaction force between price and quantity may be introduced.

These force accounts may be accumulated across periods, but a treatment analogous to capital accounts may be adopted by aggregating balances at the end of a period into summary accounts similar to retained earnings in capital accounts.

Amounts attributable to force accounts may be determined at the end of a period all at once, but they may also be determined throughout the period by matching a certain flow with another flow.

Note that unlike temporal triple-entry bookkeeping, force accounts here are not a mirror image of capital accounts nor wealth accounts. Only the relationship between force accounts and capital accounts is a mirror image of the relationship between capital accounts and wealth accounts.

In any event, a static evaluation of an enterprise is not unimportant but is incomplete. This is why wealth accounts alone cannot show a full picture of the financial status of an enterprise. Its dynamic behavior is a crucial element in such an evaluation, for which income accounts have served an indispensable function.

But in order to describe the dynamic behavior of a moving system, a description of its position and velocity at a given point in time alone is not complete. The acceleration, that is the rate at which the velocity is changing, is essential information to describe the behavior properly.

Currently, an internal or external evaluation of an enterprise is based only on the information presented in balance sheet, income and funds statements. Since the acceleration concept is not developed in these statements, users of the statements must take into account the acceleration by themselves, resulting in, for example, different price-earnings ratios.

The force accounts are designed to present such data gathered in an objective and systematic manner. In the above, a simple example of a force statement was presented. Let us now consider a slightly more detailed statement.

# 4. Statement of Force

## 4.1 Three Statements

While it is easy to conceptually develop various types of force accounts, it takes considerable time and effort to experiment alternative accounts to see which are most useful. It takes even more time and effort to establish accounting principles or standards that will govern the recording and reporting of force accounts in relation to wealth and capital accounts. After all it took five centuries for accountants to develop the present level of concepts, principles and standards that govern wealth and capital accounts. What is described below is only a brief outline of what force accounts and force statements may look like.

Before proceeding on a design of a force statement, it is important to understand the relationship between wealth and capital accounts and the way in which they are reflected in financial statements. Then, analogy can take us easily to an understanding of what the new statement should be.

Wealth accounts are summarized in balance sheet. However, balance sheet contains capital accounts. Therefore, let us call a statement "wealth statement" when it is obtained from balance sheet by eliminating capital accounts. It lists all assets and all liabilities, arriving at total wealth as shown in Table 4-1.

**Table 4-1:** Wealth Statement

| | | |
|---|---|---|
| Assets | | |
| Current Assets | $90 | |
| Long-term Assets | 80 | $170 |
| Liabilities | | |
| Current Liabilities | -10 | |
| Long-term Liabilities | -40 | -50 |
| Total Wealth | | $120 |

Capital accounts are mostly reflected in income statement. It is, however, incomplete as a statement representing all changes in wealth, since such things as new stock issues are not included. Therefore, let us consider "capital statement" which includes income statement, other changes in retained earnings (currently shown in statement of changes in retained earnings), and changes in other capital accounts (which appear in statement of changes in owners' equity).

Entries in funds statement are either already reflected in capital accounts or they are fund-nonfund or nonfund-nonfund transfers that do not affect total wealth. Here, the term fund is used to mean net working capital, which is current assets less current liabilities. While nonfund-nonfund transfers do not affect funds, they are included in conventional funds statement from the viewpoint of representing movements of all financial resources.   Analogously, such transfers may be introduced in capital statement to reflect not only changes in total wealth but also changes in the composition of wealth.   Their effects on total wealth, however, should cancel each other.   A sample of capital statement is shown in Table 4-2.

**Table 4-2:**  Capital Statement

| | | |
|---|---:|---:|
| Beginning Wealth | | $75 |
| Income | | |
|   Revenues | $70 | |
|   Cost of Sales | -20 | |
|   Other Expenses | -5 | |
|   Net Income | | 45 |
| Dividends Declared | | - |
| New Stock Issues | | - |
| Ending Wealth | | $120 |

Although capital statement summarizes all flows that contributed to wealth change, it must begin with a stock entry.   That stock entry should be beginning wealth which is, of course, equal to beginning capital.   This entry, which serves like a constant of integration in calculus, is introduced so that the sum of capital accounts is equal to the sum of wealth accounts.   It establishes the initial condition, so to speak, for operations in this period.

Let us now examine force statement.   It must start with two items that establish initial conditions for operations in this period.   One is beginning wealth just as it is used in capital statement.   It establishes the amount of stock which existed at the beginning.   The other is beginning income momentum, which is the rate of income that existed at the beginning.   The two, together, show what the total wealth would have been at end, had there been no forces existing in the operations during the period.

After the first two items, the structure of the remaining accounts is made in a more flexible way depending upon the need for information.   The simplest arrangement might be to take the difference between this year's income items and the corresponding items in the last year.

For example, a skeleton form of a force statement might look like the one shown in Table 4-3, assuming that income is the only item that affected total wealth.   Then, in this table, "Increase in Income" may be classified in more detail using income accounts as a basis, such as increase in revenue, increase in cost of sales, increase in operating expense, etc.

While force attributed to this year can be listed as a change in each income

**Table 4-3:** Force Statement

| | | |
|---|---:|---:|
| Beginning Wealth | | $75 |
| Last Year's Income | $25 | |
| Increase in Income | 20 | |
| This Year's Income | | 45 |
| Ending Wealth | | $120 |

account over last year, this type of listing is not likely to be very useful. It is analogous to preparing income statement simply by listing the difference between ending and beginning balances of each asset and liability account.

To create a useful income statement, a more careful classification is needed.

## 4.2 Force Statement and Variance Analysis

Instead of presenting a listing of income accounts whose amounts are merely differences between this year and last year, the change in income may be decomposed into fixed and variable components. The variable component may further be decomposed into price and quantity components.

For example, a force statement may be presented as shown in Table 4-4

**Table 4-4:** Force Statement and Variance Analysis

| | | |
|---|---:|---:|
| Beginning Wealth | | $75 |
| Beginning Income Momentum | $25 | |
| Changes in Income Momentum | | |
| Attributable to Forces on: | | |
| Selling price | 20 | |
| Variable cost | -10 | |
| Sales volume | 8 | |
| Fixed cost | 2 | |
| Ending Income Momentum | | 45 |
| Ending Wealth | | $120 |

. This example shows that the company earned $45 in income this year, which is the sole reason for the change in wealth since no dividends were declared and no other capital transactions existed. Out of $45, $25 was judged to be attributable to income momentum already existing at the beginning of the year; hence, this portion of income is attributed to prior years' activities.

For simplicity, let us assume that this amount -- $25 -- is exactly equal to last year's income, as if the momentum never decayed. The remaining $20 is attributed to the force exerted this year. An increase in selling price, from $5/unit last year to $7/unit this year, contributed an additional income of $20 evaluated at this year's volume of 10 units. Unit variable cost also increased from $1/unit to $2/unit. This reduced income by $10, that is, the unit cost increase of $1 multiplied by this year's volume of 10 units.

This year's sales volume of 10 units was more than last year's 8 units and when this increased volume of 2 units is multiplied by last year's margin ($4 which is $5 less $1), income increase attributable to sales volume change is figured to be $8. There was a decrease in fixed cost from $7 last year to $5 this year, resulting in a $2 increase in income. All of these completely account for the changes in income momentum between this year and last year as clearly shown in the table above.

Additional concepts may gradually be introduced in a force statement. For example, a rate of decay in income momentum may be explicitly introduced in a manner analogous to depreciation rates. Such a decay rate may be called a *friction* rate, characterizing the environment in which business operations take place. Suppose in the above example, a friction rate of 50% is applicable to sales volume so that only a half of last year's sales volume is expected to be realized this year in the absence of this year's sales efforts. Hence, income momentum attributable to prior years is only 4 units times $4 margin, less $7 fixed cost; namely, $9 instead of $25 shown before, or a reduction of $16. Changes in income momentum this year, attributed to the force exerted on sales volume, however, will be increased by the corresponding amount ($16), making it $24.

## 4.3 Recurring and Nonrecurring Forces

Just as income is classified into ordinary and extraordinary income, force applied this year may be classified into recurring and nonrecurring (or in further details based on the estimated decay rates). Recurring force is the one that increases not only income this year but also in the future years, while nonrecurring force is the one that increases income only this year. Nonrecurring force boosts income once to a higher level where income will stay in the absence of friction and other forces. Recurring force keeps pushing income to a higher and higher level. In most case, force is nonrecurring. But in some cases it may be proper to recognize the recurring nature of force. For example, once a cost-of-living adjustment in wage is signed with a union, its income effect takes place not just in one year but continues so long as inflation lasts.

Strictly speaking, the effect of force must be evaluated in terms of *impulse*, which is force times duration of time during which the force is exerted. It is, however, convenient to consider whether the force, whatever its duration may be, is exerted recurringly or only for one duration that expires within a period.

Such a classification of force into recurring and nonrecurring is actually a matter that belongs to the fourth dimension of this differential multiple-entry bookkeeping, since it accounts for changes in force. However, there is nothing wrong in reflecting it in this statement of the third dimension, for a better use and forecast of the items in the force statement. A classification of income into ordinary and extraordinary income definitely belongs to the issue to be covered in the third dimension; this classification has done no harm to income statement but rather improved its usefulness. The same may be said of classification of force along this line.

The kind of variance analysis presented in Table 4-4 may be carried out to a much finer level. For example, sales may be analyzed into (1) sales to continuing customers and (2) sales to new customers; where the former is attributed to last year's force while the latter is attributed to force applied this year. Ultimately, however, such a judgment on force may be carried out on a transaction-by-transaction basis and can be made an integral part of a journal entry, under which every journal entry has three columns.

Intra-wealth transactions such as purchases of inventories, may have no entries in the second and the third column, since they have no impact on income nor on force. However, once a transaction changes net wealth, its impact needs to be explained not only by an income account in the second column but also by a force account in the third column. This is necessary to express the accountant's judgment on which wealth accounts were affected, which income accounts can explain the reasons for the change, and which forces are responsible for the income. In this way, every income item is properly "accounted for" by force accounts just as wealth items are accounted for by income accounts in double-entry bookkeeping.

It is also important to recognize that the measurement of force is carried out by means of the measurement of income which, in turn, depends upon the measurement of wealth. Therefore, the measurement basis, such as historical cost, current cost, etc., used in measuring wealth, has a critical impact on the way in which income and force are measured.

Undoubtedly, a recording of changes in income momentum on the transaction-by-transaction is far more difficult than their periodic assessment, but so is a recording of wealth changes on the same basis in the double-entry system. Accountants have developed a number of simplifying assumptions to enable them to carry out the recording of the transactions in a systematic manner. For example, the historical cost principle allows them to focus only on particular transactions that caused an acquisition and a disposal of a given good since, during the period in which the good is held in the enterprise, its value is assumed to remain at the acquisition cost. An analogy suggests that no changes in income momentum are assumed unless there is an evidence via actual transactions that the momentum has shifted. Thus, for example, sales in an earlier part of a given period will be attributed to the sales momentum existing at the beginning of the period; but toward the end of the period cumulative sales may clearly suggest a change in the momentum, at which point the sales may begin to be attributed to a different force which presumably has caused such a change.

## **4.4** Friction

The next question is what portion of the change in this year's income over last year's is attributable to this year's (or prior year's) activities. In wealth accounts, the most important figure is aggregate wealth; namely, assets less liabilities, which represents the bookvalue of the enterprise. In capital accounts, the most important figure is net income -- the amount of wealth increase attributable to this year's activities. In the same way, in force accounts, the most important figure is net force of the year, which is the increase in net income attributable to the year's activities.

Just as bookvalue-per-share or earnings-per-share has been widely quoted and used in analysis, force-per-share can become an important figure in assessing the enterprise's future profitability. Force-per-share can indicate how much earnings-per-share was increased this year over the last year as a result of this year's activities.

The underlying idea is that not all of this year's income is the contribution made by activities this year. Once a customer is acquired, orders can come in automatically or with some "maintenance" cost that is not as high as the cost of acquiring the customer. Then, not all income arising out of this year's orders from the customer would be attributed to this year.

The key measurement that is needed here is the rate of "friction" which causes the income momentum to decay. Let us express the friction rate as a fraction of income that must be lost from one year to the next. It is like depreciation rate under the declining balance method, except that the depreciation rate is applied to assets while the friction rate is applied to income.

Zero friction rate implies an environment where customers will keep buying at the same rate, where prices will remain the same, where expenses will be incurred at the same rate, etc., unless the momentum is disturbed by forces exerted in this year. Normally, however, a positive fraction is called for as a measure of the friction.

Like depreciation or overhead allocation, this is one of the crucial areas where accountant's judgment will be called for. Various methods on accounting for frictions, such as straight-line, sum-of-years-digit, double-declining balance method, may be considered along with an estimate of life expectancy of income momentum. In the above discussion, the friction rate is said to apply to income. However, it is certainly possible to apply separate rates for various revenues and expense accounts. Determining life expectancy of revenues or expenses and their decay patterns under various conditions will be the most important task in developing this new force dimension.

# 5. Calculus of Accounting

## 5.1 Dynamic Patterns of Growth

Once information on wealth, income, and force becomes a regular part of financial statements, much more advanced techniques may be introduced in using the information. From information on wealth and income alone, only some elementary ratio analyses have been possible. With more detailed information on force, the acceleration or deceleration of income can be intelligently analyzed.

Dynamic patterns of a firm's growth may be analyzed utilizing various tools that have been developed in growth theory in economics. In turn, individual company data can provide useful input to economic analyses, especially on the studies of the impact of firms' growth on the pattern of industry or national growth as well as the studies of the impact on the size distributions and concentration measures in industry or in the economy [20].

Calculus of finite differences can become an important tool of financial analysis, since using information on wealth, income and force, various difference equations may be hypothesized and tested to describe the growth pattern of an enterprise. Such analyses can in turn sharpen the accountants' classification of forces and attribution of income changes to them.

In fact, a whole new field of what may be called *calculus of accounting* may be developed so as to integrate accounting measurements closely with mathematical and economic concepts and theories. Calculus of accounting will not be a mere reproduction or translation of concepts and theories in other fields but will reflect the accounting environment both in measurements and their uses for dynamic analyses of a business enterprise.

What is presented below is only an introductory example of how a measurement of force may be related to valuing a company. Explanation is made in the least mathematical way using a numerical example.

Before proceeding further, it may be pointed out that in mechanics force is a concept abstracted from observations of an object's acceleration. When force is applied to an object, the result is an acceleration of the object. From the measurement standpoint, therefore, it is easier to discuss acceleration than force. Only after acceleration is measured and its portions properly attributed to various contributing forces, the measurement of force becomes feasible. Thus, in the following example, the term "(income) acceleration" will be used without specifying which force is responsible for it.

In discussing the growth pattern of a company's wealth, it is convenient to consider such terms as "wealth," "income," or "income acceleration" on the per-share basis. Thus the following concepts and notations will be used:

- $\omega$ Wealth or bookvalue (per share)

- $\pi$ Income Momentum (per share per year)

- $\alpha$ Income Acceleration (per share per year per year)

## **5.2** Capitalization of Income

Now consider two companies with the same bookvalue at $40 a share; namely, $\omega$ = $40. On the balance sheet, these two companies might look exactly alike. Yet, economically they may be of totally different value because of the difference in their earning power. If Company A earns $8 per share ($\pi_A$ = $8) and Company B earns $4 per share ($\pi_B$ = $4), A's rate of return (on bookvalue) is 20% while B's is only 10%. This difference is bound to be reflected as the difference in their stock prices. If price-earnings ratio of 10 is considered to be reasonable for the type of industry that the two companies are in, and for the type of financial structure that the two companies have, then A will be selling at $80 a share, or twice as large as the bookvalue, while B is selling at $40 a share, or at its bookvalue.

If their indicated wealth is the same, why is there a difference? Certainly, a part of the difficulty lies in the measurement system especially in the historical cost principle; under the principle prices used to value wealth may be prices observed many years or decades ago.

Attempts to remedy this problem have been under way, both in theory and in practice. Adjustments on wealth and income due to price changes have been based (a) on historical cost adjusted for general price-level change and also, (b) on current cost. In the United States, it is now required to disclose the effect on income of adjustments under both bases.

Yet neither method can remedy the fundamental deficiency in the way in which wealth is measured. Current measurements of wealth are almost all static, piece-by-piece measurements: static, in the sense that the measurement reflects its price at one point in time, either current, historical, or price-level adjusted historical; piece-by-piece, in the sense that each component of the whole wealth is measured and then the resulting measures are added together.

Such a static approach to measuring wealth is useful in providing a fairly objective benchmark for wealth measurement, but it cannot be sufficient because wealth is also dynamic, as Irving Fisher emphasized. Income is a derivative of wealth, but as far as measurement goes, wealth is determined from income via its capitalization, according to Fisher [10].

If the capitalization rate of 10% a year (the reciprocal of price-earnings ratio or earnings multiple) is reasonable, an $8-a-year income stream lasting forever (a perpetual income stream) has a present value of $80; and the same for a $4-a-year stream has a present value of only $40, assuming that income occurs at the end of each year beginning a year from now. The reason its present value is $80 may be seen from the fact that if one has $80 in cash and a bank accepts it as a deposit on which interest is paid at 10% a year, an income stream of $8 a year can be generated forever; hence, the perpetuity of $8 a year and present cash of $80 are equivalent. The same holds for the $4-a-year perpetuity and present cash of $40.

Strictly speaking, calculating present value makes sense only when discounting is applied to cash flows and not when it is applied to income, since the latter is the result of not only operating cash flows but also depreciation and other non-cash items. However, when contemplating an infinite stream of income as a bench mark, it may be acceptable to consider cash flows and income flows interchangeably on the assumption that depreciation and other non-cash items are negligible, due, for example, to indefinite lives of properties.

## **5.3** Capitalization of Income Acceleration

Let us now shift the argument one level higher in the hierarchy of differentials. Consider two companies both with bookvalue of $40 and income of $8 on the per-share basis. The two companies may look exactly alike, both on the balance sheet and the income statement. But suppose that Company A's income has been increasing at the rate of $2 a year while Company B's income only at $1 a year. Certainly, Company A is more likely to be selling at a higher price than Company B. A's income growth record is much better than B's; hence, A is likely to enjoy a better price-earnings ratio than B.

In evaluating income as a basis for an enterprise value, it is important to look at income in one year not in isolation, but also dynamically along with income in prior years. This is where the acceleration measure plays on important role. In this example, A's acceleration is, on the per-share basis, $2 per year per year (or $2/yr$^2$), namely income per year is increased by $2 per year, while B's acceleration is $1 per year per year (or $1/yr$^2$). What is the value of such an acceleration in income if the capitalization rate is, as before, 10% a year?

Suppose that an income stream for 19x1, 19x2, 19x3, ... is $8, $10, $12, ..., increasing at the rate of $2 a year *forever*. Its present value is to be calculated at 10% as of the end of 19x0 under the assumption that all income occurs at end of the respective period. The income stream may be divided into different layers. The first layer consists of an $8-a-year income stream beginning the end of 19x1. The second layer consists of a $2-a-year income stream beginning the end of 19x2. The third layer consists of the same $2-a-year income stream beginning the end of 19x3, and so on. (See the breakdown of income stream in Table 5-1.)

As stated before, an $8-a-year perpetual income stream beginning the end of 19x1 is worth $80 at the end of 19x0. Hence, the present value of this portion of income stream is entered under the 19x0 column as {80}, where { } means it is the present value of income stream on its right.

The $2 increase in income that occurs at the end of 19x2 creates a $2-a-year perpetual income stream beginning the end of 19x2. By the same argument used in evaluating the $8 income stream, this $2 income stream is worth $20 evaluated at the end of 19x1. (That is, $20 deposited at bank at 10% at the end of 19x1 can take care of all future income stream at the rate of $2 a year.) Hence, {20} is placed under the 19x1 column.

In this way, it may be seen that the perpetual income stream of $8, $10, $12,

**Table 5-1:** Income Stream and Its Present Value

|  |  | 19x0 | 19x1 | 19x2 | 19x3 | 19x4 | 19x5 |  |
|---|---|---|---|---|---|---|---|---|
| Income Stream |  |  |  | 8 | 10 | 12 | 14 | 16 | ... |
| Attributed to |  |  |  |  |  |  |  |  |
|  | 19x1 | {80} | 8 | 8 | 8 | 8 | 8 | ... |
|  | 19x2 |  | {20} | 2 | 2 | 2 | 2 | ... |
|  | 19x3 |  |  | {20} | 2 | 2 | 2 | ... |
|  | 19x4 |  |  |  | {20} | 2 | 2 | ... |
|  | 19x5 |  |  |  |  | {20} | 2 | ... |
|  |  | {{200}} | {20} | {20} | {20} | {20} | {20} | ... |
| Total Present Value |  | 280 |  |  |  |  |  |  |

$14, $16, ... is financially equivalent to another perpetual income stream of $20, $20, $20, ..., plus the present value of $80 for the first layer.

Applying the same capitalization argument again on the $20-a-year income stream, it is worth $200. Hence, the entire income stream of $8, $10, $12, $14, $16, ... is worth $200 + $80 = $280 at 10% rate of capitalization.

Once the principle is understood, it is simple to use a short cut. An $8-a-year income stream is worth $80, obtained by $\pi/r$ where $r = .1$ is the rate of capitalization expressed in fraction and $\pi$ is per-share income. A $2-a-year-a-year acceleration, however, creates a $20-a-year income stream, obtained by $\alpha/r$ where $\alpha = \$2/\text{yr}^2$ is the acceleration. The $20-a-year income stream is in turn worth $200, obtained by $[\alpha/r]/r = \alpha/r^2$.

If instead of the capitalization rate (10%) the use of its reciprocal, earnings multiple (10), is preferred, then current income stream of $8 a year is valued by multiplying it by 10, while the acceleration of $2/yr$^2$ is valued at $2 times 10 times 10 or $2 times the square of the earnings multiple.

Although in Table 5-1, it was assumed that the $8-a-year income stream begins a year from the base point (year-end 19x0), and the $2-a-year income acceleration begins two years from the base point, it is a simple matter of multiplying the total present value, such as $280 computed above, by $1 + r$ which is 1.1 in the above example, if the income stream starts immediately and the acceleration effect starts one year from the base point.

## 5.4 Decay of Force

Needless to say, a force that accelerates income at the constant amount forever is meaningful only in a conceptual world, since its effect normally decays. Suppose that the rate of force decay (denoted by $\nu$) is 40%. This means in the above example that income is increased by $2 in 19x2 but only 60% of $2 or $1.20 in 19x3. Similarly, income in 19x4 increased only by 60% of

$1.20 or $.72. Hence, the income stream is not $8, $10, $12, $14, $16,... but $8, $10, $11.20 $11.92, $12.352,.... What is the present value of this income stream when the capitalization rate is 10%?

The answer is very simple. First, looking at Table 5-1 above, the first layer of the $8-a-year stream beginning 19x1 and the next layer of the $2-a-year stream beginning 19x2 remain the same as before. But the third layer of income stream beginning 19x3 is no longer $2 a year but only $1.20 a year. Hence, the present value at 19x2 is not {20} as shown in the table, but {12}. Applying the same argument, the next layer is $.72 a year, hence, its present value at 19x3 should be {7.2}.

If we set aside the present value of the first layer which is {80} as before, the income stream aggregated by layers is not {20}, {20}, {20}, {20},... but {20}, {12}, {7.2}, {4.32},... The present value of this latter stream is simply $40, obtained by dividing the first item, 20, by the sum (.5) of the capitalization rate $(r = .1)$ and the decay rate $(\nu = .4)$ for the reason that will be explained below.

Suppose that one deposits $40 in a bank at 10%; it grows to $44 at the end of the first year. By paying $20, all of the $2-a-year income stream that is on the second layer of the table can be taken care of, since this stream is worth $20 as indicated by {20}.

This leaves $24, which is 60% of $40, the amount one started out with. But, having taken care of the first item {20}, the remaining aggregate income series [{12}, {7.2}, {4.32},...] that needs to be taken care of is exactly 60% of the original series [{20}, {12}, {7.2},...]. Thus, while the principal amount shrunk from 40 to 24 by 40%, the income series that must be taken care of by the principal also declined by exactly the same percentage. Hence, the process can be repeated in perpetuity.

Thus, in general, if the decay rate is $\nu$, a force that created an acceleration $\alpha/yr^2$ in its first year is worth $[\alpha/r]/(r + \nu) = \alpha/\{r(r + \nu)\}$. If $\nu = 0$, the formula goes back to the non-decay case discussed earlier, in which the force is worth $\alpha/r^2$.

As the decay rate changes from 0, .1, .2, ..., .9, to 1, the present value of income streams (setting aside the first layer which is worth {80}) is reduced as follows (rounded to the nearest whole number):

| Friction rate | 0 | .1 | .2 | .3 | .4 | .5 | .6 | .7 | .8 | .9 | 1.0 |
|---|---|---|---|---|---|---|---|---|---|---|---|
| Present Value | 200 | 100 | 67 | 50 | 40 | 33 | 29 | 25 | 22 | 20 | 18 |

The last case is the same as having only the layer of a $2-a-year income stream beginning 19x2 with other layers diminished due to the 100% decay. The present value of the $2-a-year stream evaluated at the end of 19x1 is shown as {20} in the above table. Since all present values are finally evaluated to the end of 19x0, $20 is further discounted by 10%, obtaining 20/1.1 = 18 approximately, as shown in the above chart. (Note that $80 must be added to each of the above to obtain the total present value comparable to the $280 figure discussed in the constant acceleration case.)

## **5.5** Friction Rate

So far it has been assumed that the enterprise operates in a frictionless world in the sense that once income is established it lasts forever. Suppose that the friction rate of 30% is applicable ($\mu = .3$). This means that the first layer of income in the above table is not 8, 8, 8, 8, ... but 8, 5.6, 3.92, 2.744,... losing 30% of the previous year's income each year. Therefore, applying the above argument, it can easily be seen that the present value of this income stream is not 8/.1 =80 as before but 8/(.1 + .3) = 20, or a multiple of only 2.5 times income.

The friction rate ($\mu$) and the force decay rate ($\nu$) can be combined in evaluating the effect of a force ($\alpha$). The stream of declining present values {20}, {12}, {7.2},... is worth 20/(.1 + .4) = 40, as calculated before, when the force decays at the rate of 40% a year. But the present value of each layer must now be reduced. For example, the second layer of a $2-a-year income stream is replaced by a stream of 2, 1.4, .98, .686,... whose present value is not 2/.1 = 20 but 2/(.1 + .3) = 5, or one-fourth of what it was before. The third layer starts with $1.2 instead of $2 due to the 40% decay in acceleration. The friction reduces this, year after year, at the rate of 30%. Hence, the stream is 1.4, .98, .686,... whose present value at 19x2 is not 1.4/.1 = 14 but 1.4/(.1 + .3) = 3.5 or one-fourth of what it was without friction.

In this way, the present value of each layer is exactly one-fourth of the value without friction. In the case of no friction, the total present value of {20}, {12}, {7.2},... is calculated as 20/(.1 + .4) = 40. Since each present value is now one-fourth of what it was before, the total present value must be (20/4)/(.1 + .4) = 10, or only five times the initial $2 effect of the force.

This process of arriving at $10 may be recapped as follows: first, the $2 effect of force is divided by the sum of the capitalization rate, r = .1, and the friction rate of $\mu = .3$, arriving at the present value of $2/(.1 + .3) = $5, or $\alpha/(r + \mu)$ (this establishes the beginning layer, the second layer in the table, of the effect of the force); this is then divided by .1 + .4 to arrive at the total present value of $10 stated above. Namely, $\alpha/(r + \mu)$ is further divided by the sum of the capitalization rate, r = .1, and the force decay rate, $\nu = .4$, obtaining $[\alpha/(r + \mu)]/(r + \nu)$.

Thus, in summary, when the friction rate of $\mu$ is applicable to the income and the decay rate of $\nu$ is applicable to the force, present value $I$ of income, $\pi$, and the present value $A$ of income acceleration are given by:

$$I = \pi/(r + \mu) \tag{11}$$

$$A = \alpha/[(r + \mu)(r + \nu)] \tag{12}$$

At a 30% friction rate, an income stream that starts out at $8 a share is worth only $20. In addition, if the force decays at the rate of 40% a year, a force whose initial effect is to increase income by $2 a year is worth only $2/[(.1 + .3)(.1 + .4)] = $10, for a total value of $30 (instead of $280 computed in the case of the frictionless world with no decay in the effect of the force).

The above is only one of numerous potential uses of acceleration measurements. The above approach using infinite series was chosen because of the simplicity of the formula and its interpretation. Cases with finite lives are much more complex, since as mathematicians say, infinity is the principle and finite is an exception. However, this approach alone may be sufficient to get a feel of the significance of measurements of acceleration and force in financial and managerial evaluation of an enterprise.

# 6. Improving Accountability

## 6.1 The Accountability Approach

It seems to be useful at this point to consider whether it would be worthwhile, both from theoretical and practical standpoints, to engage in the development of a triple-entry bookkeeping system, now that the nature of its third dimension has been identified, the budget and force statements have been outlined, and the use of a force measurement has been considered.

As pointed out earlier, neither the budget dimension in temporal triple-entry bookkeeping nor the force dimension in differential triple-entry bookkeeping is new to accounting. Planning and budgeting have been an integral part of management accounting, and comparisons and analyses of actual versus budget have been observed widely both in theory and in practice. Similarly, variance analyses between this year's results and last year's, in terms of revenues, expenses, gains and losses, also have been adapted widely in theory as well as in practice.

The key point of potential contributions by triple-entry bookkeeping must thus lie in the fact that the new systems of triple-entry bookkeeping make such analyses systematic, complete, and integrated with conventional accounting. If these analyses are carried out under a triple-entry system, they will become more systematic than before, since they will be placed under the rigorous set of principles and standards of accounting. They will not be fragmentary analyses but will be complete, since otherwise the triple-entry equation cannot be satisfied. They will become not isolated analyses but an integral part of bookkeeping that includes conventional dimensions, principles, standards, and accounts.

From the standpoint of supplying information useful for decision making, unsystematic, incomplete, and unintegrated analyses of budget versus actual, or this year's flows versus last years flows, might not be a problem. The integrated approach provides more comprehensive data, but it is costly. For the use in decision-making alone, the cost-benefit trade-off may or may not be favorable toward actually implementing such a system.

However, to view accounting as a system of supplying information useful for decision-making is only one approach. Along with it, there is another important approach to accounting which may be called the *accountability* approach. Pros and cons of implementing a triple-entry system must therefore be considered from this standpoint, too.

This accountability approach has been elaborated in Ijiri (1975) [17] and contrasted with the decision approach which is currently the widespread view of accounting. The following is a brief summary of the contrast between the two approaches:

1) Under the decision approach, the objective of accounting is to provide information useful in economic decision-making. This approach emphasizes the contents of financial statements instead of the accounting system that lies

behind the statements. Furthermore, this approach depicts accountants merely as servants to the decision maker. Finally, this approach neglects possible reactions from the system whose performance is measured and reported to the decision maker. These will be discussed in turn.

2) The accountability approach recognizes, not the two parties (the decision maker and the accountant) as in the decision approach, but three parties: the *accountor*, the *accountee*, and the *accountant*. An accountability relationship is created between the accountor and the accountee via a variety of instruments, such as a constitution, a law, a regulation, a contract, an organizational rule, a custom, or by an informal ethical obligation. Whatever the accountability relationship may be, the accountor is accountable to the accountee for his or her activities and their consequences under the relationship. This accountability relationship normally requires an accountor to account for his or her activities and their consequences by keeping records and reporting the summary information to the accountee. The accountant, then, joins as a third party in this accountability relationship so that the charges and discharges of account-ability can function smoothly between the accountor and the accountee.

In contrast to the decision approach, the accountability approach considers the system behind financial statements rather than statements per se. This is because the objective of accounting can be achieved even if the accountee never reads financial statements insofar as the accounting system helps the accountor behave accountably. Needless to say, under the decision approach, accounting fails to achieve its objective if the decision maker does not read financial statements or any other information generated by the system.

Secondly, the accountant is not a servant to the decision maker in the accountability approach, but is a person acting as an intermediary between the accountor and the accountee. The need for objective, neutral, unbiased information cannot be understood from the decision standpoint alone; if the accountant were to serve only a single master, such things as subjectivity or biasedness of information will not be a problem insofar as it generates a profitable result to the decision maker. Requirements for objective and unbiased information can only make sense when the accountant is placed between two parties having conflict of interest with respect to the contents of the accounting information.

As a consequence, the accountability approach recognizes the accountor's interest in the contents of information flowing to the accountee and possible attempts by the accountor to influence the contents in his favor. For this reason, this approach emphasizes not just objective measures that people can agree when their interest is not affected by the measure, but rather "hard" measures that people find difficult to dispute even if they know that their interest is going to be directly affected by the measure.

## **6.2** Accounting for the Future

Having emphasized the accountability approach to accounting, the revelation that the duality underlying the double-entry system may be viewed as present = past was a particularly welcoming surprise. If this interpretation is reasonable, this means that double-entry bookkeeping impounds at its base the notion of accountability. That is, as stated before, the double-entry system is essentially a way of "accounting for the present by the past." The present wealth is not just measured and reported to a decision maker but is "accounted for" by the past flows that caused the change.

Consider the power of a triple-entry system that insists on getting future events accounted for in a similar fashion (temporal triple-entry bookkeeping) or getting the reasons for changes in income accounted for (differential triple-entry bookkeeping). Under a single-entry system, changes in wealth can be recorded in an isolated manner so that if there were stock losses or errors in recording, they can be fixed easily within a single account. The pressure to look into the reasons for the gain or loss is not there because nonstandard simple descriptions are sufficient for recording any transactions.

The same is not true with a double-entry system. An increase or decrease in wealth cannot be recorded. It must have a standardized "explanation" in the form of a capital account. Furthermore, such a matching of accounts means that one's judgment on this explanation will be out in the open for many people to see and examine, since the matter goes beyond a single account or a single ledger.

This is a considerable pressure, especially because accountants must make the judgment not just at the year-end when statements are prepared, but also day after day every time they record a journal entry. Like French gender or Japanese seniority that is built in at the root of their respective languages, double-entry bookkeeping has accountability impounded at the heart of accounting so that those who do not pay respect to it cannot even speak the language or record in a journal entry.

Consider a similar pressure that a temporal triple-entry system may bring about. A journal entry under the system means that a wealth change must not only be explained by a capital account, but also be accounted for vis-a-vis budgets. Every sales or every expense must be attributed to a budget account. If it is totally unexpected and cannot be attributed to any of the budget items prepared at the beginning of the year, it may be attributed to a budget account designated to capture unexpected events. But this is done only after existing accounts are examined and judged to be not suitable. In this way, accountability that has been oriented almost exclusively toward the past can be oriented toward the future under this temporal triple-entry system.

## **6.3** Accounting for the Force

While the power of temporal triple-entry bookkeeping is significant in extending our horizon toward the future, the power of differential triple-entry bookkeeping is even more significant in extending our ability to reason to a higher level. It calls for reasons for reasons. If a wealth change is attributed to a proper income account which explains the reason for the change, then an income change relative to last year must be attributed to a proper force account which explains the reason for the change. Think of the pressure that may be placed on the accountants' ability to reason, especially in view of its unrelentless existence in their daily life if every journal entry is to include force accounts. Think of the value of the extended ability if such an ability is to become second nature to accountants in the future, an ability to reason a cause of income change and attribute it to a proper force among numerous forces that exist in and out of an enterprise.

This may sounds like a fantasy but actually is not. After five hundred years of practicing double-entry bookkeeping, the ability to reason a cause of wealth change and to attribute it to a proper income account has become second nature to anyone who calls himself or herself an accountant. In fact, the difficulty in learning double-entry bookkeeping is not because the mechanics are complex, but the ability to find a reason for a wealth change must be acquired. This ability is also what distinguishes accountants in the double-entry era from those in the single-entry era who were under no pressure to develop such an ability.

The power of a language (including a bookkeeping system) to influence our perception and reasoning should not be underestimated. A linguistic authority, Edward Sapir [36], describes this power elegantly:

> Human beings do not live in the objective world alone, nor alone in the world of social activity as ordinarily understood, but are very much at the mercy of the particular language which has become the medium of expression for their society. It is quite an illusion to imagine that one adjusts to reality essentially without the use of language and that language is merely an incidental means of solving specific problems of communication or reflection. The fact of the matter is that the "real world" is to a large extent unconsciously built up on the language habits of the group (pp. 209-10).

If force is one of the dimension of the accounting language, it will become an integral part of accountants' and managers' thinking, just as income has already become an indispensable element in every phase of business. Considering the power that double-entry bookkeeping has had in impounding the notion of income in the minds of accountants and managers, Sombart's following statement [37] may not be an exaggeration.

> One can scarcely conceive of capitalism without double-entry book-keeping: they are related as are form and content. It is difficult to decide, however, whether in double-entry book-keeping capitalism provided itself with a tool to make it more effective, or whether capitalism derives from the "spirit" of double-entry book-keeping (Vol. II, Part I, p. 118).

If under the triple-entry system income changes are systematically and completely accounted for by a set of accounts representing various forces inside and outside of a business enterprise, the impact of such a practice on business can be just as profound as the impact of double-entry bookkeeping. This is the challenge open to accountants in the three dimensional world.

## **6.4** Science and Politics

Before leaving the subject of accountability, it seems to be important to emphasize the distinction between accounting as a branch of science and accounting as an instrument of politics. The emphasis on the accountability approach elaborated above should *not* be taken to mean that more accountability is always preferred to less.

Like everything else, cost is always associated with accountability. Accountability means that people engaged in productive activities must be partially diverted to do something for someone else's benefit; this diversion will not directly contribute to productivity, although, hopefully, the time diverted for accountability will eventually return in the form of more productivity from the societal standpoint.

Whether the current level of accountability should be made higher or lower is a question of politics. Recently, financial disclosure requirements imposed upon corporations have been a topic of controversy. Undoubtedly, accounting information has been traded in the arena of politics where it is determined who should disclose what and when.

As some advocates say, it may indeed be true that we are living in the world of over-accountability. This is, in part, the result of the loss of mutual trust among various constituencies in the financial world.

But whether over-accountability or under-accountability, it has nothing to do with the *science of accounting*. Conceptual and technical discoveries must be pursued for the sake of scientific curiosity, if for no other reason. It would be nice to have new developments accepted and implemented in practice but that would be secondary (from the scientific standpoint) to the primary task of understanding accounting phenomena.

Therefore, those who try to reduce accountability should not be critical of the triple-entry system per se; however, they are certainly free to oppose its implementation in any specific areas because of cost or other reasons.

# 7. Accounting in the Third Dimension

## 7.1 Beyond Triple-Entry Bookkeeping

In summary, it has been shown that the perfectness hypothesis of double-entry bookkeeping turned out to be false. It is possible to extend it on the time horizon to temporal triple-entry bookkeeping and also to extend it on the differential horizon to differential triple-entry bookkeeping. Both of them are extensions from the same framework of double-entry bookkeeping extended in different directions.

They both preserve the existing double-entry system but extend it to include a third dimension. The third dimension selected under each of the two interpretations of the existing two dimensions is respectively unique and is a logical extension of the two.

Would it be possible to extend these triple-entry bookkeeping systems beyond triple entry? Temporal triple-entry bookkeeping appears to be inextensible since the trichotomy of past, present, and future seems to be so natural that any attempt to extend it to quadruple-entry bookkeeping is likely to destroy the internal logic that binds the three dimensions.

Differential triple-entry bookkeeping is, however, a different story. These is no reason why the search for a new dimension should stop at three. A fourth dimension can easily be introduced at least in theory, to account for changes in force. A series of differentiation can naturally and logically extend to infinity.

One may wonder why such an extension into the fourth and higher dimensions did not occur in Newtonian mechanics. This is stated in physics as, for example, French [11] says;

> As far as kinematics by itself is concerned, there is no good reason why we should stop here. We could define and evaluate the rate of change of acceleration, but in general this does not represent information of any basic physical interest, and so our discussion of mechanics is based almost exclusively on the three quantities, displacement, velocity, and acceleration (p. 86).

In accounting, however, the concept of change in force seems to be a meaningful one. Force may be classified into recurring force, which is expected to be continually effective in further increasing income next year, and into nonrecurring force, which is not expected to recur next year. When the concept of force is more firmly established in practice, it would be possible to define and measure change in force as entries in the fourth dimension of a quadruple-entry system.

In addition, it is certainly conceivable, at least theoretically, to combine a temporal triple-entry system with a differential multiple-entry system, under which the bookkeeping equation extends indefinitely in both directions, past and future:

$$....\textbf{Potential} = \textbf{Budget} = \textbf{Wealth} = \textbf{Capital} = \textbf{Force}.... \qquad (13)$$

The term potential is used here to designate the mirror image of the force dimension when it is reflected toward the direction of the future.

Furthermore, there is no reason why temporal and differential triple-entry bookkeeping are the only possible extensions of double-entry bookkeeping. Hence an interesting question: Is there any other way of developing a triple-entry system that satisfies the preservation and integrity conditions stated earlier?

It will be interesting to explore this issue, not just because it might lead to another attractive triple-entry bookkeeping system but also because it is likely to suggest a new insight into the bookkeeping systems that have not been normally considered.

## **7.2** Causal Double-Entry Bookkeeping

There is, however, a problem that appears to be the most difficult one to solve in dealing with double-entry bookkeeping. To explain this, it is necessary to discuss a distinction between two types of double-entry bookkeeping that were introduced in Ijiri (1967) [15]. They are called *classificational* double entry and *causal* double entry.

In an entry such as [debit Cash, credit Capital], the equality of debit and credit occurs because the same set of objects are classified in two different ways. Thus, assets = equities for no reason other than that the same total amount is classified in two different ways, one based on physical-economic properties of assets and the other based on claims on them.

An entry such as [debit Inventories, credit Cash] has a totally different reason why the equality should hold. Here, it is not because the same set of objects is classified in two different ways (since inventories and cash are different things), but the amount of inventories obtained is *set equal to* the amount of cash foregone, for the reason that the two are causally linked together. This is nothing but a form to express the *historical cost principle.* Inventories may actually be worth more or less than the amount of cash given up, but under this principle it is defined to be equal.

This distinction between the two types of double entry has not been made in the literature of double-entry bookkeeping. For example, Pacioli [30] explains such transactions as "debit Palermo Sugar, credit Cash" as if they were conceptually no different from such entries as "debit Cash, credit Capital." The two are, however, conceptually quite different. The latter transaction involving wealth and capital accounts is legitimately recorded in two columns because it stems from the basic wealth-capital dichotomy, while the former involving two wealth accounts is spread over two columns merely to avoid a negative number.

The equality in causal double entry expresses a matching of an increment and a decrement; namely,

$$\textbf{Increment = Decrement} \tag{14}$$

While the same equality sign is used, the meaning of this equality is totally different from the equality in earlier equations 1 through 4. Earlier equalities are mathematical *identities* because, by virtue of the fact that both sides of the equality are two classifications of the same set of objects, the equality can never be violated. By definition the two are equal; or in other words it is an identity.

The equality in equation 14 is not because the two sides of the equality are intrinsically equal, but because the historical cost convention forces the two to be equal.

The equality in equation 14 can better be expressed as

$$\textbf{Increment} \twoheadleftarrow \textbf{Decrement} \tag{15}$$

The $\twoheadleftarrow$ is used to mean an *assignment* in computer programming. It means that the amount of the item on the left side of the arrow is *set equal to* the amount of the item on the right side of the arrow.

An expression for this causal double entry, however, may be stated at least in a form comparable to earlier equations expressing classificational double entry if the increment and the decrement are put on the same side of the quality, since they are both changes in the same category, wealth; namely,

$$\textbf{Increment - Decrement} = \textbf{0} \tag{16}$$

Transactions of this type were discussed earlier in Section 2.2 as intra-wealth or intra-capital transactions that do not affect total wealth nor total capital. Such intra-dimensional transactions have been recorded, as shown in Table 2.2, in journal entries whose total for each dimension is zero. Under the existing double-entry bookkeeping system, these transactions are entered in each of two dimensions (a debit entry and a credit entry) in order to avoid negative entries, as discussed in Section 1.4.

If statistics on all journal entries under the existing double-entry bookkeeping system were available, they might show that while a significant portion -- let us say half of the journal entries -- would be classificational (that is, inter-dimensional such as an entry [debit Cash, credit Income]), the other important half would be causal (that is, intra-dimensional such as an entry [debit Inventories, credit Cash].) Therefore, although it has been demonstrated in this monograph that classificational double-entry bookkeeping can indeed be extended to triple- and in general multiple-entry bookkeeping, it remains to be shown whether or not causal double-entry bookkeeping can also be extended to triple- or multiple-entry bookkeeping.

## 7.3 Three-Valued Logic

Let us now consider the contrast between Increment and Decrement and see whether it makes any sense to add a third item to the equality via

$$\textbf{Increment} = \textbf{Decrement} = \textbf{?} \tag{17}$$

Applied to the specific example of a cash purchase mentioned above, this equation means [debit Inventories, credit Cash, and ?].

The dichotomy of increment versus decrement seems to stem from our fundamental two-valued logic. At the heart of our logic we have only two states (0 and 1, for example, using a binary representation in computer) and only two ways of recognizing a change -- a plus (moving from 0 to 1) or a minus (moving from 1 to 0). Therefore, this increment-decrement duality seems to defy any attempt to introduce a third item in a natural, logical manner. This difficulty in extending causal double entry to a triple-entry system is described in Ijiri (1975) [17], considering such things as "many-valued logic [35]."

For this reason, this monograph has presented a proof of imperfectness and extensibility of double-entry bookkeeping in only "half" of its territory. The other half of double-entry bookkeeping still appears to be formidably perfect.

Indeed, it is quite possible that the praises, quoted in Section 1.1, by notable persons in the history of double-entry bookkeeping were actually directed toward this perfect half. But then, since causal double-entry is only a form to express the substance, that is the historical cost principle, would it not be possible that these praises were misdirected toward double-entry bookkeeping when they were in fact aimed at the historical cost principle behind double-entry bookkeeping?

Such misdirected praises are quite reasonable because, until this century, virtually all bookkeeping was done under the historical cost principle; hence, the distinction between the form (the double-entry system) and the substance (the historical cost principle) were unnecessary. (See an elaboration of this viewpoint using a dialogue format in Ijiri (1981) [19].)

In any event, to disprove the perfectness hypothesis for causal double-entry appears to be an extremely difficult task, mainly because the binary logic seems to be buried in the heart of our thinking. A creature from another planet, perhaps a tri-sexual species with three-valued logic built into its chromosomes, might possibly be able to come up with a true (causal) triple-entry system. But if so, how will it be able to communicate the result to us?

There is a related issue in this regard. That is whether there is a triple-entry bookkeeping system that is perfect in the sense that it cannot be extended to a quadruple-entry bookkeeping system without destroying its internal logic. In the above analysis, it has been found that temporal triple-entry bookkeeping is not a true triple-entry system but rather a double-entry system applied twice; also, differential triple-entry bookkeeping can be extended indefinitely by continually adding a new dimension generated from the derivative of the last dimension. Neither of them, therefore, is perfect for different reasons.

Note that in the differential triple-entry system the third dimension relates to the second dimension in exactly the same way that the second dimension relates to the first dimension; hence, the same relation may be used to generate the fourth and higher dimensions. If, however, it is possible to discover a trichotomy in which the third relates to the second, the second relates to the first, *and* the first relates to the third, all in exactly the same way, then it might offer a basis upon which a perfect triple-entry system can be constructed.

Whether such a system can actually be developed, with or without the aid of three-valued logic, remains to be explored.

## **7.4** Implementation of Triple-Entry Bookkeeping

While there are many interesting issues to be explored on the theoretical structure of bookkeeping as discussed above, there are numerous problems that must be resolved in implementing the two types of triple-entry bookkeeping elaborated on in this monograph. It may perhaps be worthwhile to discuss some approaches to implementing such systems of bookkeeping.

Temporal triple-entry bookkeeping is much easier to implement than differential triple-entry bookkeeping because the concept and the measurement of budget, which is the core of the third dimension in this triple-entry system, are widely accepted in practice.

Undoubtedly, many corporations must be using some forms of budget statements that incorporate in part the issues discussed in the monograph. (For example, according to James L. Murdy, Senior Vice President of Gulf Oil Corporation, a system of management reports had been developed under his initiative, which is partially in line with the approach underlying the temporal triple-entry bookkeeping system discussed above.)

Therefore, perhaps the first step toward implementing a temporal triple-entry system is to develop a standardized form of an integrated financial statement that accommodates the three dimensions -- budget, wealth and capital. The use of such a statement will hopefully be accepted in practice beginning with internal management reports and extending to external financial reports.

However, financial statements and management reports alone will not be sufficient. Financial records, including journal entries, must incorporate the budget dimension. A model of such entries needs to be developed for a small company as a prototype and to be extended to accommodate complex transactions involving consolidation, foreign exchange, and inflation accounting. Existing financial accounting standards must also be extended to cover the budget dimension. If the articulation of balance sheet and income statement is considered to be desirable, so is the articulation of the three dimensions -- budget, wealth, and capital -- in this integrated financial statement. But such an articulation can be achieved only when consistent accounting standards are applied to all three dimensions.

On the theoretical front, this means a streamlining of theories and practices that, heretofore, developed independently in different fields of accounting, notably financial accounting, management accounting, and fund accounting. Temporal triple-entry bookkeeping offers a framework under which various theories, principles, and standards may be integrated.

Development of differential triple-entry bookkeeping is significantly more difficult, mainly because it requires a set of new concepts, accounts, and measurements in the third dimension that has not been explored before. Perhaps the best way of implementing this triple-entry system is to take a small company as a prototype and to concentrate on identifying and measuring "income momentum." Various revenues and expenses should be classified into recurring and nonrecurring items. The patterns of decay in recurring items must be observed. After having developed a reasonable basis for measurement of income momentum, changes in income momentum may then be analyzed and attributed to specific forces that exist in and out of the enterprise.

On the theoretical front, accounting models of an enterprise may be developed using the concept of force and its effect on income momentum. Such models may serve as a target toward which the actual accounting measurement system is directed. They may also offer a basis for integrating theories on the behavior of an enterprise that have been developed in economics, finance, and accounting.

It is exciting to realize that such a virgin territory as triple-entry bookkeeping and related accounting in the third dimension is wide open to accountants in the twentieth century and beyond.

# REFERENCES

**1.** Abs, George *et at.* "Historical Dates in Accounting." *The Accounting Review XXIX*, 3 (July 1954), pp. 486-493.

**2.** American Accounting Association Executive Committee. "A Tentative Set of Accounting Principles Affecting Corporate Reports." *The Accounting Review XI*, 3 (June 1936), pp. 187-191.

**3.** American Institute of Certified Public Accountants, the Study Group on the Objectives of Financial Statements. *Objectives of Financial Statements.* American Institute of CPAs, 1973.

**4.** Cajori, F. *A History of Mathematics.* MacMillan, 1919.

**5.** Cayley, Arthur. *The Principles of Bookkeeping by Double Entry.* Cambridge University Press, England, 1894.

**6.** Cooper, W.W., Dopuch, N., and Keller, T.F. "Budgetary Disclosure." *The Accounting Review XLIII*, 3 (July 1968), pp. 640-648.

**7.** Davidson, S. "Publication of Budgets: A Forward Step". In B.A. Zaidi, Ed., *Reporting in the Seventies*, California Center for Research and Management Services, California State University, 1972, pp. 1-18.

**8.** deRoover, Raymond. "Characteristics of Bookkeeping Before Paciolo." *The Accounting Review XIII*, 2 (June 1938), pp. 144-149.

**9.** _____ . "The Development of Accounting Prior to Luca Pacioli According to the Account-books of Medieval Merchants". In Littleton, A.C. and B.S. Yamey, Ed., *Studies in the History of Accounting*, Irwin, 1956, pp. 114-174.

**10.** Fisher, Irving. *The Nature of Capital and Income.* Macmillan, 1906.

**11.** French, A.P. *Newtonian Mechanics.* W.W. Norton & Co., 1971.

**12.** Goethe, Johann von. *Wilhelm Meister's Apprenticeship and Travels.* Chapman and Hall, London, 1824. Translated by Thomas Carlyle.

**13.** Hain, H.P. "Accounting Control in the Zenon Papyri." *The Accounting Review XLI*, 4 (October 1966), pp. 699-703.

**14.** Ijiri, Yuji. "Physical Measures and Multi-Dimensional Accounting". In R.K. Jaedicke, Y. Ijiri, and O. Nielsen, Ed., *Research in Accounting Measurement*, American Accounting Association, 1966, pp. 150-164.

**15.** _____. *The Foundations of Accounting Measurement.* Prentice-Hall, 1967.

**16.** _____. "Budgetary Principles and Budget-Auditing Standards." *The Accounting Review XLIII*, 3 (July 1968), pp. 662-667.

**17.** _____. *Theory of Accounting Measurement.* American Accounting Association, 1975.

**18.** _____. "An Introduction to Corporate Accounting Standards: A Review." *The Accounting Review LV*, 4 (October 1980), pp. 620-628.

**19.** _____. *Historical Cost Accounting and Its Rationality.* Canadian Certified General Accountants Association, 1981.

**20.** _____ and Simon, Herbert A. *Skew Distributions and the Sizes of Business Firms.* North-Holland, 1977.

**21.** Johnson, Howard P. "Triple-Entry Bookkeeping: An Answer to Internal Revenue Service ADP." *Taxes-The Tax Magazine XLI* (March 1963), pp. 168-174.

**22.** _____. "The Investment Credit and Triple Entries." *Taxes-The Tax Magazine XLI* (June 1963), pp. 331-336.

**23.** Keister, Orville R. "Commercial Record-Keeping in Ancient Mesopotamia." *The Accounting Review XXXVIII*, 2 (April 1963), pp. 371-376.

**24.** Kline, M. *Mathematical Thought from Ancient to Modern Times.* Oxford University Press, 1972.

**25.** Kohler, Eric L. *A Dictionary for Accountants.* Prentice-Hall, 1952. Sixth Edition Edited by William W. Cooper and Yuji Ijiri, published in 1982.

**26.** Littleton, A.C. "Paciolo and Modern Accounting." *The Accounting Review III*, 3 (June 1928), pp. 131-140.

**27.** _____. *Accounting Evolution to 1900.* American Institute Publishing Co., 1933.

**28.** _____. "The Accounting Exchange." *The Accounting Review XX*, 3 (July 1945), pp. 348-359.

**29.** Mattessich, R. "Toward a General and Axiomatic Foundation of Accountancy -- With an Introduction to the Matrix Formulation of Accounting Systems." *Accounting Research VIII*, 4 (October 1957), pp. 328-355.

**30.** Pacioli, Luca. *Summa de Artithmetica, Geometria, Proportioni et Proportionalita: Distintio Nona-Tractatus XI, Particularis de computis et scripturis.* Paganino de Paganini, Venice, 1494. Translated by R.G. Brown and K.S. Johnston in *Paciolo on Accounting*, McGraw-Hill, 1963

**31.** Paton, W.A. "Theory of the Double-Entry System." *Journal of Accountancy XXIII*, 1 (January 1917), pp. 7-26.

**32.** Paton, William A. and Littleton, A.C. *An Introduction to Corporate Accounting Standards.* American Accounting Association, 1940.

**33.** Peragallo, Edward. *Origin and Evoluation of Double Entry Bookkeeping.* American Institute Publishing Co., 1938.

**34.** Peters, R.M., and Emery, D.R. "The Role of Negative Numbers in the Development of Double Entry Bookkeeping." *Journal of Accounting Research XVI*, 2 (Autumn 1978), pp. 424-426.

**35.** Rosser, J.B. and Turquette, A.R. *Many-Valued Logics.* North-Holland, 1958.

**36.** Sapir, Edward. "The Status of Linguistics as a Science." *Language V* (1929), pp. 207-214.

**37.** Sombart, Werner. *Der moderne Kapitalismus.* Dunker und Humbolt, Munchen and Leipzig, 1928. Sixth Edition.

**38.** Yamey, Basil S. *Essays on the History of Accounting.* Arno Press, 1978.